The Unbreakable Athlete

Ironman Edition

The Unbreakable Athlete

IRONMAN

Injury Prevention

By T. J. Murphy

Published by Meyer & Meyer Sport

British Library Cataloguing in Publication Data
A catalogue record for this book is available from the British Library

T. J. Murphy
The Unbreakable Athlete — Injury Prevention
Ironman
Oxford: Meyer & Meyer Sport (UK) Ltd., 2005
ISBN 1-84126-109-2

© 2005 by Meyer & Meyer Sport (UK) Ltd.
Aachen, Adelaide, Auckland, Budapest, Graz, Johannesburg,
New York, Olten (CH), Oxford, Singapore, Toronto
Member of the World
Sports Publishers' Association (WSPA)
www.w-s-p-a.org
Printed and bound by: FINIDR, s. r. o.,Český Těšín
ISBN 1-84126-109-2
E-Mail: verlag@m-m-sports.com
www.m-m-sports.com

Contents

PART II: THE UNBREAKABLE SPIRIT

Acknowledgements

For their tremendous support over the years and the opportunity to write freely about the heart and soul of triathlon, a very special thank you to Kelly Mione and Fran Arfaras, my editors and friends at Ironmanlive.com.

For their great spirit and dedication to the sport, thanks to the great staff at Triathlete Magazine, a team I'm lucky and proud to be a part of.

And for the opportunity to be their editorial voice in San Francisco, thanks to Bob Babbitt, Lois Schwartz and John Smith at Competitor Publishing.

"You might think you know your limits, but you don't. You won't find out what you've really got to offer until you're really pushed to the brink, and even then you can do more than you think. You find this a lot in this sport and it's why there's a delicate balance between what your body can deliver and what your mind thinks you've got. At times your mind can run off with your body and you really pay. The main thing you learn in this sport is that there are going to be times when you feel absolutely miserable, but it's part of the experience; and if you keep working, things will turn around ... you just have to keep plowing along."

— Tim Twietmeyer,
five-time winner
of the Western States 100

Introduction

The golden rule of triathlon says that success is staked more in consisistency than motivation. Once you've caught the triathlon bug, motivation is easy. Triathlon is the easiest sport in the world to overtrain for. Triathletes burn out all the time. To fulfill your potential as a triathlete requires you to spread your desire evenly across the days, months and years in what often seems a never-ending sequence of workouts. The thing that often gets in the way, sending you packing back several squares, is an injury or illness, or a weakness of commitment when challenged by the day-after-day effort required regardless of weather or mood.

For those enjoying longevity in triathlon, many have learned a number of critical lessons the hard way. More than a basic injury prevention book, this book seeks to present below-the-surface lessons with the hope that those new to the sport can learn from mistakes that have caused countless strains, pulls and slides into the heavy depths of overtraining.

But this book strives to go beyond the physical. Equally important, and far more important in regard to the Ironman triathlon, is the unbreakable mind and the undeniable spirit. Being out on the course for 10 or more hours hands you over to a battle with inner demons and weaknesses at a time when you're most vulnerable.

In addition to tips and techniques, this book, using stories from the race course, is intended to be a roadmap to the deeper strengths that exist within us all.

PART I
INJURY PREVENTION

Chapter 1

Lessons Learned the Hard Way

THAT DON'T HAVE TO BE LEARNED THE HARD WAY

1.1 Temper Enthusiasm

A top triathlon coach once said to me — stealing from a saying about crashes in cycling — there are two types of distance runners: those who have had a running injury and those who *will* have a running injury.

There's nothing more energizing for a runner than to look at a well-crafted training plan on which you are about to embark. It could be six weeks, 12 weeks, 24 weeks, or a year or multi-year plan. Common components include long runs, base mileage, threshold runs, track workouts, Fartlek, easy runs, weight training, stretching, and on and on. If it's your first training plan, such a written plan can be particularly inspiring because you feel you're looking at a launch into the world of high fitness. If you're experienced, the excitement lies within chasing a new time goal, a new distance to be covered, or the goal of beating someone else. Regardless, it's fun to pour through and imagine the future.

What you'll never see in a training plan, whether you've drafted it from a book, torn it out of the pages of a magazine, or paid a coach to write it for you, are injuries that may well be lurking out in the future, tripping you at week three or week 10. Generally speaking, one of the prices you pay to be an athlete is that there are no guarantees against getting injured. Any athlete who thinks he or she can't get hurt is probably the most likely to end up getting hurt.

Those new to running or triathlon have probably heard something about this, but the likely fact is that they didn't register it nor really believe it. Over and over, it has to be learned the hard way. A friend of mine by the name of Marla was a perfect example. I was living in New York at the time and training for the Ironman Triathlon World Championship (in the following referred to as Hawaii Ironman) in 2000. Marla approached me about how to take up running and, as all runners are, I was happy to answer her questions and make suggestions on how she should start. Also, like most veteran runners (and coaches), I know that I'll never have all the answers, and anyone who says they have all the answers should be avoided at all costs. Still, considering my experience and relative ability, Marla would have been smart to listen to me.

I'd told Marla that the key to successfully getting a running program off the ground was to start slow and with a low amount of mileage. For her, I figured two to three times a week at 20-30 minutes would be plenty. I suggested that it'd be best if she kept it to two runs a week and added some cross-training — biking would be perfect — once or twice a week. I said sticking with a simple program like that for 3-4 weeks would be a tremendous start; she had zero athletic background (she was in her mid-20s), and starting gently like this would give her bones, muscles, and tendons a chance to be exposed to the new stress and gradually adapt by getting stronger. If she followed a cautious schedule, she could lessen the chance of injury, and increase her progress. I also recommended buying a good pair of running shoes.

Marla went out for her first run and ran as far as she could as fast as she could. She wore retro Pumas because she was too excited to wait until she could make it to a running shoe store. She reported to me that night, blazing with enthusiasm about her new life as a runner. She was fine, she said, and knew that she could handle running every day. I listened to her and tried to emphasize that she needed to take a breath, listen to me and adhere to a patient, meditative schedule. I told her that enjoyment of the exercise could swiftly be taken away by overzealousness. I told her about how there are elite distance runners who log 140 miles a week and more, much of it at mind-boggling paces, but that it took each and every one of them years and years and years to train their bodies to handle such incredible volume. As a beginner with weak muscles, tendons, and ligaments, damage could strike like lightning.

I hung up the phone, knowing that she didn't believe me. Sure enough, two days later, she called and told me about the shin splints she had, the aching Achilles tendon, the sore muscles. She couldn't even try to run for another week, and I'm pretty sure she gave up completely, because I never heard from her again.

It left me thinking about what could have happened. If Marla had followed the sketch of the training plan I'd given to her, it's far less likely she would have met with such discouraging results so soon. It would have been more likely that she would have tasted the satisfaction of the best part about being an endurance athlete: the satisfaction of a ritualistic discipline that leans toward conservative long-term goals rather than high-ledged short-term goals that are risky.

Lessons that shouldn't have to be learned the hard way:

New runners and triathletes should never trust themselves to know how much training they can or can't do. In other words, get instruction. Good instruction best comes from a qualified coach or from a good book.

Listen to your coach. Like a devil on the shoulder, your enthusiasm from early success will try and talk you into doing more training than you're being counseled to. If you tame this tendency and listen to your coach, you'll have saved yourself years of learning this lesson the hard way.

1.2 Beware Feelings of Invincibility

Last chapter, we talked about the more obvious and easy-to-understand pitfall that beginners fall into, that of being impatient at the beginning. It should be noted that a similar pitfall also hinders plenty of experienced athletes, for a different reason.

About 10 years ago, I was mid-way through a track season in which I was focusing on the 1500-meter run. I was coming off a breakthrough cross-country season, my first, and after spending the previous several years focusing on the marathon, through a lot of good training, I'd sprung free some 5k speed. That spring, I was making good progress going into distances I hadn't run since around 1980, when I was in high school. I matched my best time as a high school 800-meter runner at the age of 30, and the season was just beginning to roll. My 1500-meter time went from 4:12 to 4:10 to 4:08, and on a warm day at the Fresno Relays, I ran 4:06. My coach said that my training was indicating I was prepared to run 4:00 flat.

In the morning runs and throughout all the track workouts and distance runs on weekends, I'd begun to feel invincible. I followed my coach's workout plans to the letter, thrashing myself with certain speed-endurance workouts that would have been unfathomable to me a year before. I felt incredibly strong. I began to make choices that reflected that: I switched from racing flats to track spikes for the track workouts. I pushed last miles in tempo runs up a little harder than they needed to be. I did my tempo workouts on the track instead of on the road or trail. I snuck in weight training workouts. I felt like I could digest it all, and that I'd just get stronger and stronger.

It was after I'd finished the 4:06 in Fresno that I first felt something stir the left hamstring. It was just a little bit tender as I jogged a warm down. I was scheduled to run an 800-meter leg in a distance medley that same afternoon. I jogged, tried stretching, and paid a visit to the first aid station for some ice.

I warmed up for the distance medley and still felt a slight twinge, but the feeling of invincibility had me convinced I could be run over by a truck and still race. As if it was all a matter of the mind.

The 400-meter runner passed me the baton, and I began my two-lap effort around the track. On the turns, I felt a grinding sensation in my hamstring. I ran a good split for me, right around 2 minutes flat, but as I walked off the track trying to get my breath, I knew that I'd shredded the leg.

The next day, my hamstring was so sore I could barely walk. I used ice on an almost hourly basis for the next couple of days. I saw a physical therapist for treatment.

When I could handle it, I got a massage. But I wouldn't be able to jog for about 10 days, and by the time I could actually run on it again, I was starting from square one to get back the fitness I'd lost.

The lesson you don't have to learn the hard way:

Beware feelings of invincibility. When you are peaking into top fitness, it is an extremely vulnerable time.

Referring back to my twist on what matter of mind means, I'm suggesting that the flood of confidence that comes with making great progress in running is laced with booby traps. You work hard and the progress comes, and you get even more fired up than you were at the start.

The golden rules are as follows:

▲ When you start to get fit or peak, increase your degree of caution to an extremely high level.

▲ At the slightest twinge of muscle or tendon discomfort, back off and tell your coach about it. End the session right there at the slightest sign that you're on the cusp of an overuse injury. Take a day or two away from the sport and do some gentle cross training. Ice the suspect area. If you're worried about losing fitness because of this, consider how much fitness you'll lose if you get injured and consider yourself lucky. If you can afford it, talk to a sports medicine professional for advice on how to preemptively treat the area.

1.3 Think Before You Drop

For different reasons, the temptation to drop out dances through every endurance athlete's brain at one point or another. Therein lies the reason we like the challenge of the endurance contest in the first place: to test our inner mettle. Sometimes dropping out is the smart thing to do; other times it carries with it the risk of psychological injury, a far more difficult problem to recover from than many physical injuries.

Do drop out from a race if injury pain is telling you that you're doing damage. In particular, this applies to long-distance triathletes or ultra runners who are exposing themselves to a hot sun and humid conditions. Simply said, heat injury can leave you in a coma, and it can even kill you. If you aren't too far gone, you can stop at an aid station, drink fluids, eat pretzels, and recover until you can walk/jog your way in, preferably after a doctor's OK. But none of this is worth dying for, and you just don't mess around with hyponatremia or heat stroke.

When it's musculo-skeletal injury pain, like a smarting Achilles tendon or knee pain or the like, the best judgement call is to play it safe. Sometimes it's just an odd little pain that is meaningless and evaporates on its own; other times it blossoms into a sharp twinge, cramp, or crack, and you won't be able to keep running even if you want.

Don't drop out from a race if you're just not racing well and are feeling discouraged. Race to the end the best that you can. Carry this directive out with the notion that you'll earn self-respect for finishing up even a bad day. You'll get tougher, and you'll have taken a step to preparing for the next race. You will have saved the day.

A good friend of mine, a fellow marathoner, trained hard and was one of the toughest runners I knew. But I recall clearly how one particularly nasty 10k, he dropped out at the half-way mark. He did it again at a marathon, and later it seemed like every race he ran he dropped out from. Endurance athletics is a tough business, and the faster you get, the more mental toughness you'll need to get through the last quarter of any race, regardless of distance. Give in to mental weakness just once, and you'll be running a huge deficit that will take a long and hard climb to erase.

Here's the thing: If you succumb to the voice in your head telling you to quit just because it doesn't feel good, then you will have made it extremely easy to drop out the next time. The flip side is that not dropping out from a race just because you feel off is as strong a habit as dropping out.

Just remember that even the greats have bad days. Bob Kempainen, a two-time Olympic marathoner and sub-2:10 marathoner, was running great until the final three months before the 1996 Olympics in Atlanta. Kempainen was adhering to a high-mileage training program, as anyone aspiring to medal in the marathon at the Olympics must, and fell victim to a mysterious lower back problem that was so bad he couldn't even run in the pool. He was forced to take weeks off, and by the time Atlanta rolled around, he was just getting back into sync. He raced (you don't skip the Olympics), but had run an extremely slow time for him, finishing well out of sight of any medal regardless of color. Afterward, he commented that the pain and effort it took to run a marathon when not completely fit far outweighs the pain of racing a much faster time when fit. But Kempainen finished. He knows that not finishing a race because of discomfort exacts a heavy price.

After you get across the finish line, take the pain with you and turn it into focus and energy to train well for the next one. Use it as psychic fuel to get to the starting line as highly prepared and healthy as possible, so that you can use all your powers to race up to your expectations.

Treat races with hot-blooded intent. Train so hard (but be careful of overtraining!) that it makes the race feel easy.

1.4 Balance
Self-Sufficience

Distance running saved my butt. While I had dabbled in running in high school, and survived a half-Ironman at 21, I didn't really get anything out of it until 1989, the year I first finished a marathon, the Big Sur Marathon. Before that, I'd failed in college, failed in the U.S. Army, and was generally flailing at anything I was trying to do at the time.

The reason Big Sur delivered some much-needed confidence and knowledge to my life was that I had followed a training plan to complete it. Rather than just hacking my way through it with a bare minimum of effort, I purchased Jeff Galloway's *Book of Running* and followed his plan for completing a marathon targeted at a time of 3:20.

Lucky for me, I was following a plan that required a commitment of six months rather than six weeks, and what I learned within that time frame was the value of slowly and humbly plodding toward a goal. There was no way to achieve the goal by being slick, or lucky, or extra talented, or knowing the right people. It required doing the work. By doing the work, I equipped myself to tackle the problem of completing a race that — in my case — I truly didn't know if I could do or not. I didn't believe I could do it until I actually crossed the line.

I followed Galloway's program and was fortunate enough at the time to live near a good running shoe store, Hoy's Sports in San Francisco. There, I was sold a good, quality pair of technical running shoes. Buying a fresh pair of shoes became a small yet treasured moment, a symbol that I was doing the training and doing it on my own. I was learning the value of a methodical and patient work ethic, which is the one universal currency that the world of endurance athletics accepts.

The world of distance running is actually counter to the concept portrayed by Alan Sillitoe's *Loneliness of the Long Distance Runner*. You might be alone when you go for a long run, but it doesn't necessarily mean you're lonely. Experienced runners get this. Having time to yourself on a training run is refreshing and addictive. Through this process of ritual and training, the endurance athlete builds a keen self-reliance built of self-motivation and a growing wariness about the way the rest of the world works.

To the veteran endurance athlete, the outer world beyond the quiet realm of self-reliance is a place frying itself with commercialism, quick-rich schemes, talking heads and incessant advertising. Through every channel of communication, it seems like someone's trying to plug his sales pitch into your head. You retreat back to your training and your training logs, and the hunger for it grows. It's the one place that seems real in our flash media world. You can feel your internal strength grow. Self-reliance deepens.

It's a great thing, one just about every distance athlete who has put some time into it learns to draw energy from. Reciprocal to the growing strength is a mistrust of experts that you shouldn't cut yourself off from, as many athletes have done over the ages. While skepticism is a good thing, there are going to be times in our athletic careers that we should seek advice and counsel from coaches, doctors, nutritionists and the like. At the elite level of triathlon, just about everyone is using the kind of team approach that cycling great Lance Armstrong uses. Armstrong finds the best minds he can in the realms of coaching, bike technology and restoration.

In other words, the by-product of self-reliance is an invaluable tool in not just becoming a good runner or triathlete, but in any pursuit. However, we must strive to avoid falling into the trap of thinking we have it all figured out.

This especially applies to preventing injuries and dealing with the trickier injuries. Sometimes ice and aspirin do the job, but injuries involving delicate structural imbalances, for example, usually need the experienced eye of a good sports medicine professional to ferret out the cause and repair the problem. There's a heady pride attached to "running through" an injury, and sometimes this can be accomplished. Other times, it's the back alley to disaster. One of the more phenomenal distance runners I've ever known is an ultra runner by the name of Gary Hilliard. I used to sell him shoes (he needed many) at Hoy's Sports after I began working there. Gary logged gargantuan amounts of miles early in the morning and after he got off his shifts working as a steel worker. I ran with him once in the Golden Gate Headlands in Marin. Gary had run 12 miles to meet the group. Together, we ran 24 miles. Then Gary ran home, another 12, for a solid 48 miles. He did most of his running in the pre-dawn, before he went off to work. He also owned a treadmill so that he could get in extra miles when he watched TV.

His races of choice were six-day races, ultra events where the winner is the one who runs the most miles in a six-day period, usually around a track or one-mile loop. Gary averaged 112 miles a day in one such event that he won. Once, when he was in the store, I asked Gary about his approach to getting past injuries; surely someone of his rank and experience had some incredible techniques.

"I'm not the one to ask about healing injuries," Gary said. "I ignore them."

About a year later, a mutual friend told me that Gary had to give up his ultra running because he'd tried to run through a classic case of sciatica, otherwise known as lower back pain. Gary pushed himself through it, and the injury pushed back. Gary lost the battle and had to give up long distance for a matter of years.

Gary's experience was the ultimate example of the sharpness of both sides of a double-edged sword.

The lesson that doesn't have to be learned the hard way:

Balance mental tenacity and self-discipline by seeking out experts you can trust. Learn to listen, without ego, to their advice.

1.5 Nutrition Counts

Train all you want, but without effective recovery and restoration, hard training doesn't mean zip. It's when you're resting and eating well that your body responds to the training stimulus with improvement. Simply put, rest means getting enough sleep and managing the stresses of life efficiently. The other biggie in the restoration equation is nutrition.

Nutrition has become amazingly complicated. Mostly because of the reams of bad information being generated to sell me and you all sorts of expensive but useless things. There's plenty of good, untainted information, as well. Nutritionists, such as Nancy Clark and Ellen Coleman, write great books that should be on every triathlete's bookshelf.

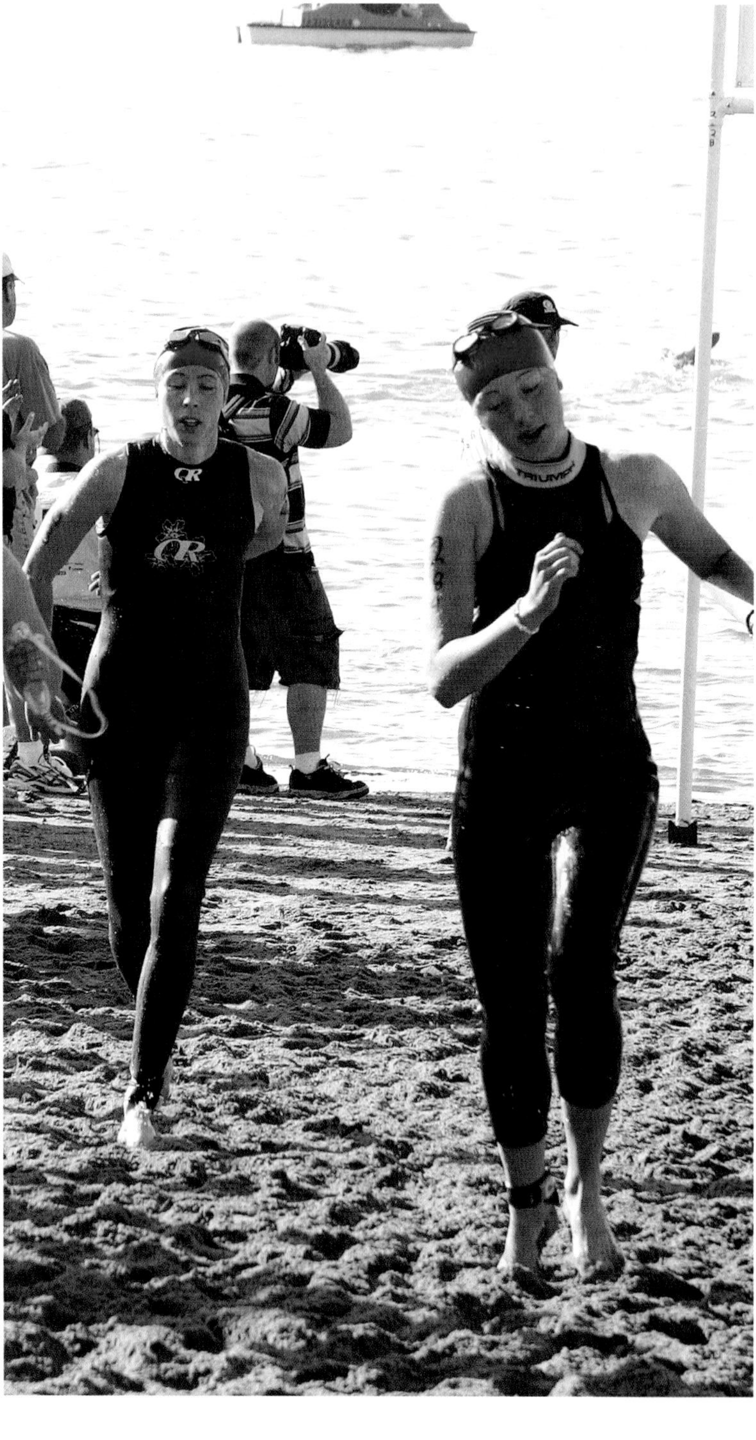
TRIUMPH

But the best way I've ever come across to really get why nutrition is so important is to experience it. Spend a week doing the following common sense things: eat a diet of whole grains, fish, fruits, vegetables and lean meats, devoid of processed foods, coffee and alcohol, and do that 100% for one or two weeks. The way you view the shelves of the grocery store, radically alters. Do that for a week or two, then go to the store, and all you see is bad food in bright packaging. Do that for a week or two, and you start feeling so good your daily cravings for sugar, salty, or fatty foods (or whatever turns you on) diminishes. It all starts looking gross.

What I recommend is a nutritional adventure to discover the simple truths involved in good nutrition. Commit yourself to one or two weeks, and you'll learn a lot. Or at least, I learned a lot. Below is how I recorded my first full tilt foray into eating healthy stuff. I'm not saying that this is the sports nutrition diet a dietician would prescribe for you, I'm just sharing my discovery of the power of nutrition. It blew my mind.

Tale of a Nutritional Overhaul

People who have known me for a long time wouldn't believe it. Right now, as I type these words, I have a cup of hot green tea steaming on my desk in a black mug while lunch is cooking in the kitchen. I have a piece of fresh salmon in the broiler, a pot of organic brown rice — spiced with dulse and garlic — simmering on the stove. For breakfast, I had organic oatmeal, two slices of brown rice bread and organic fruit. I've been sipping at cold, filtered water with a twist of organic lemon throughout the day. The dinner menu looks to be burritos with organic vegetables and black beans, more brown rice and fruit for dessert.

Somewhere in the day I'll cram organic celery, apples and oranges into a Krups juice extractor and have about 10 ounces worth of beverage bubbling with enzymes. In the evening, you'll find me brewing chamomile tea. Everything I will have consumed through the course of the day will be either organic, free-range or filtered, depending on the kinship term. And, a true stunner for me, I'm hooked on my first step toward a more holistic approach to fitness and sports.

Let me now confess that for more than a decade my approach to athletics has been stuck solely in the singular dimension of aerobic exercise. At 39 years of age, I was eating the way I'd always eaten. That is to say, lunch was a sandwich and Coke, dinner was macaroni and cheese or pizza or a burger and side salad drenched in ranch, and breakfast would most likely take the form of a bagel and cream cheese and carton of orange juice.

The foundation of this breakfast was always a breathtakingly large cup of premium-grade coffee. A bucking-bronco blend of beans from Hawaii and South America, it bluntly transported a dose of caffeine that, before knocking me out with a crash, sent me on a tear at work. Sometimes I was effective and fast, sometimes I was hyper and scattered, and sometimes just tired to the bone for no obvious reason. At night, I'd fight to get to sleep — not exactly a good sign. In the morning, I'd wake up feeling wrecked. The antidote was always the first cup of coffee, and of course, a morning run.

There is a faction of thinking in the world of endurance athletics that insists diet is not extraordinarily relevant if you log enough workout mileage. In the words of running novelist John Parker Jr., "If the till is hot enough, anything will burn. Even Big Macs."

This is a corner of sports nutrition theory that I, too, have not only lived by, but fought doggedly to protect. When you're running high mileage training for a marathon, or logging upwards of 20 hours of weekly training in preparation for an Ironman, eating a doughnut feels like tossing a paper ball into an electrical fire. The body's metabolism, whipped up into a greedy panic, is ravenous for calories and doesn't seem to care if it's fats or carbs or hotdogs or beets sliding into the gullet. Coffee, beer, Pringles, and other vices burn in the rage of glycogen's flame.

Junk mileage cancels out the junk food. This was the equation I've fought to protect by not giving it much thought. Because if you look at it from any sort of scientific or common sense perch, it's a teetering sight. "You are what you eat," has more meaty common-sense credentials.

An Urgent Memo from My Body

Over the past six months, I've been plagued with a knee problem, and my running mileage slipped considerably. I wasn't getting my trusty antidote — no endorphins to wash out the complaints from my body. Still, buffalo wings were not off the menu. In other words, I was hearing but not listening.

I became aware that, except for caffeine-induced spells of energy, I felt tired and cranky. It wasn't a good tired that comes at the end of a good, solid workday. Rather, it felt more like being sick.

After admitting to myself that my unhealthy diet was slowly pushing me off a cliff, I serendipitously met a friend of mine (a marathoner and Ironman triathlete) and his wife for dinner when visiting San Diego a couple of months ago. Matt was on the tail end of a one-week fast restricted to soups and juices. We talked about fasting, what it takes and what it delivers, and it was then that my body began desperately tapping me on the shoulder with the message, "You should do that!"

Body Basics: The Things I Didn't Know

Upon my return to San Francisco, I discussed the idea of fasting for detoxification purposes with my girlfriend, who, while sharing my addiction to coffee, was far more tuned in to a good diet than I've ever been. She liked the idea too, probably due to alarm at my "food" choices while watching World Series games together.

We decided to hunt down an appropriate book on the subject. We picked the book, *Toxic Relief: Restore Health and Energy Through Fasting and Detoxification*, by Don Colbert, M.D. I found the idea of fasting intriguing, and I wanted the why and what-for explained to me in a doctor-like fashion.

That's exactly what the book gives. Spiritual aspects of fasting are left mostly for the last two chapters — from a Christian point of view — for those interested. But the first 10 chapters are focused on how to fast safely and effectively to clean out your system and introduce your body to a whole new nutritional approach.

Planet Toxin

In the first three chapters, Dr. Colbert lays down a referenced overview of the average American's intake of toxic chemicals from air and water pollution and from food — all compounded by the well-documented trend toward obesity. It's pretty terrible stuff.

Here are a few of the highlights of contamination revealed to me: lead in our bones; DDT in our fatty tissues; and 1,672,127,735 pounds of chemicals (heavy metals within the mix) released into the atmosphere in the United States in 1993. In fact, when we take in a breath of air, along with carbon monoxide and smog from autos and industry, we may be taking in a good helping of benzene, formaldehyde, vinyl chloride, toluene, carbon tetrachloride and other "volatile organic compounds," many of which can cause cancer.

Then there are pesticides — 1.2 billion pounds of which are sprayed onto our crops every year, as well as used in animal feeds for livestock.

If that's not enough, there are nitrates and chlorine in our drinking water, preservatives and bleaching agents in our food, hormone-fed meat, PCBs in fresh-water fish, and mercury, lead, cadmium, and arsenic — all non-soluble and toxic — everywhere, including the tissues of our bodies. No long run is ever going to burn these off!

There's even a condition called "Sick Building Syndrome" in which occupants of a building experience acute health effects that seem to be linked to time spent in a building, but no specific illness or cause can be identified.

And then there are folks like me, who consider French fries a serving from the fruit and vegetable group and beer a good source of vitamins.

"We may actually be starving from a nutritional standpoint while at the same time becoming grossly obese," Dr. Colbert writes. "As a result of our overindulgences we have an epidemic of heart disease, arteriosclerosis, hypertension, diabetes, cancer, allergies, obesity, arthritis, osteoporosis and a host of other painful and debilitating degenerative diseases."

The final problem, notes Colbert, is that someone who is wolfing down large amounts of "dead," nutrition-less food will continue receiving pulsed messages from the brain that the body's undernourished. Our hero then loosens up his belt another notch and raids the pantry for barbecue potato chips.

Getting on the Path: Detoxification

Reading about the detox process, the discipline required, and the benefits involved hooked me through the center. I was in.

With the objective being a spring-cleaning-like detoxification and investment in good health, Dr. Colbert's program is not just a matter of diving into a fast for a few days. Rather, he instructs readers to practice two weeks of a "liver-cleansing" diet in order to prepare for the fast. Our football-sized livers spend 24 hours a day filtering our blood, about two quarts worth per minute. The goal during this period is to decrease the flow of toxins in the diet and load up the body — in particular the liver — with nutrients and vitamins that support this work.

I scribbled into a notebook my initial shopping list of pesticide-free organics: cabbage, cauliflower, broccoli, mustard greens, turnips, beets, carrots, brown rice, wild rice, brown rice bread, brown rice crackers, extra virgin olive oil, oatmeal, avocado, salmon, free-range chicken, green tea, and a collection of various fruits. I bought garlic and dulse (a salt alternative made from seaweed).

I picked up a water filter and a juicer from the hardware store. From a health food store, I bought a range of herbal teas and vitamin supplements that Dr. Colbert recommends — a strong multi vitamin, herbal supplements, minerals to include manganese and zinc, and antioxidants, such as vitamins C and E.

The bags of organic groceries and supplements would be displacing the foods that made up a good portion of my soon-to-be-former diet. Dr. Colbert provides a list of foods to avoid. Now banned from my table for the next four weeks were processed foods, fried foods, hormone-boosted fowl and meat, fish from fish farms, alcohol, dairy products, wheat and corn products, colas, chocolate, cheese, and, the scary part, coffee.

The First Day

I started my first day with a cup of green tea instead of my old friend, a high-pitched coffee buzz. Green tea's value as an anti-oxidant, according to Dr. Colbert, is that it's 200 times more powerful than vitamin E and 500 times more potent than vitamin C.

"Green Tea is believed to block the effect of cancer-causing chemicals," he writes, adding that it gooses cancer-blocking enzymes into action.

That said, it was (at first) a sad replacement for a cup of fresh-ground brew. This day turned into an experiment in mental drowsiness. In the days to come, I would also encounter grogginess and morning headaches. However, after my first breakfast — whole-grain oatmeal with apple slices, red grapes and pecans; two slices of brown rice toast; and a glass of water to wash down prescribed vitamins and supplements — I sensed a deep rush stirring from within, almost a giddiness. In spite of the caffeine-shortage shock, I felt good.

For lunch, I had brown rice and vegetables, an apple, a pear and more water. For dinner, I lightly sauted vegetables to go along with broiled free-range chicken breast, fruit for dessert and a cup of mandarin orange herbal tea. Just prior to hitting the sack, I had a cup of chamomile tea. Before I dropped off into the deepest sleep I could ever remember, I wrote in my notebook, "Today was the most nutritious day I've ever logged on planet Earth."

Breaking Away

I continued to eat the same way for the entire "liver-cleansing" phase. It took me eight days to finally break free from the hangover left by quitting coffee. But, when I was free of it, I wanted to throw a party for myself. It was as if I was one of the star travelers in the movie *Alien* who had successfully expunged the space monster using me as a host. I was no longer hanging on for life from cup-to-cup like (to use another John L. Parker quote) "a crazed marsupial in a flash flood."

In effect, I was sleeping better and my energy was strong early in the day — and even stayed that way. No more ill-fated bungee jumps at high noon. The grogginess now a fading memory, my senses were sharper and my thinking more calm and clear.

I also began dropping pounds. Since my knee injury had plagued my training, I'd gained about 20 that I surely didn't want. By the time I was ready to start the next phase, a three-day juice fast, I'd lost six of them — without any sort of starving or deprivation.

And the biggest surprise of all: I was starting to enjoy green tea. Weird!

The Juice Fast

My girlfriend had also performed the first phase of the detox program. In person and over the phone, we'd compare notes. We were getting similar results in every department, as she, too, had left coffee behind. We took a three-day weekend to embark on the juice fast, the core ingredient in Dr. Colbert's plan to wash the body free of poisons and nasty chemicals.

Fasting, of course, is largely acquainted with spiritual and religious disciplines, from Christianity to Buddhism to Huichol Shamanism. But our project was geared for the health benefits advertised in the book. After a detailed and alarming discussion of toxins and their connection to degenerative diseases and other health problems, Dr. Colbert suggests part of the answer can be properly executed fasting.

"Fasting is a powerful, natural way to cleanse your body from the burden of excess toxic nutrients, such as bad fats, and from all other chemicals and toxins that cause degenerative diseases...It is the safest and best way to heal the body from degenerative diseases caused by being overfed with the wrong nutrition." He goes on to detail a long list of additional benefits.

Later in the chapter, he lays out his argument that, for most, a juice fast is the best way to go rather than a water-only fast. He believes that juice fasting is more beneficial because it supports the liver, breathes fresh life into the system with vitamins, phytonutrients, minerals and antioxidants, and is less stressful on the body. Like a water fast, a juice fast also gives the digestive system a huge vacation from the normal grind, allowing it time to do some deep cleaning.

Per his instructions, we planned for and began a three-day juice fast, which would be followed by a four-day breaking of the fast.

It was another illuminating journey. Using recipes from Dr. Colbert's book, like "Breakfast Drink One" (a cocktail made from juiced berries, oranges and a lime) or "Lunch Juice Five" (made from dandelion greens, celery stalks and carrots), we marched our way through the fast in kind of a happy daze. We were both surprised that we never struggled with hunger pains and noticed how the acuteness of our sense of smell went off the charts.

Throughout the day, we could drink specific teas and filtered water. In the evening, again following the instructions, we used the juicer to make soups, which we warmed on the stove. The three days passed quite smoothly, almost dreamily so. One morning, we both woke up with a metallic taste in our mouths, which we assumed might be a result of the body expelling toxins.

Then it was on to the post-fast phase — a four-day reintroduction to chewing and digesting food. On day one, we were only allowed raw fruits, like berries, apples and watermelon. On day two, we could add a simple soup at lunch and a dinner made of freshly chopped vegetables and water. By the end of the phase, we could even add a small portion of free-range chicken or meat. At this point, we were to spend the next two weeks back on the liver-cleansing diet. The mission would then be complete.

The Bottom Line

In the end, I lost more than 10 pounds. I no longer wake up looking puffy and swollen. More importantly, I feel better than I can ever remember feeling — my best evidence that I achieved a measure of toxic flush. I have more energy, a much improved sense of being, and (although I admit I'm not sure what the correlation is) I've shed a general muscular stiffness that I thought I'd been stuck with because of lots of miles and marathons. Whatever, it's gone.

I'm also pleased to report that I now eat like this all the time, save for an occasional beer or pizza. But instead of craving junk food, I'm craving all the good stuff I've been introduced to.

Quite a blanket endorsement for a holistically oriented nutrition overhaul, I know. But if you share any of my history with bad food, hot coffee and cold beer, I highly recommend either taking a look at Dr. Colbert's book, or bringing it up with a good nutrition and wellness counselor and putting together an appropriate program of your own. I guarantee it's a good buzz.

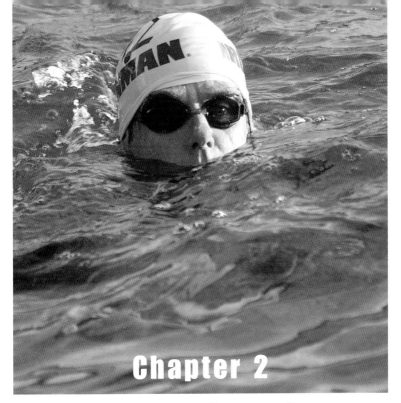

Chapter 2

Notes for the Triathlon Newbie

CHOICE BASICS TO HELP THE ASPIRING BEGINNER SAFELY GET OVER THE HUMP

2.1 Get Hooked on Exercise

The Secret Gate to Becoming a Triathlete

Not long ago, I went for a run on the Great Ocean Highway at the southwestern corner of Golden Gate Park in San Francisco.

While runners have always been a common sight at just about any time of the week on the footpath, that Saturday, the undulating pavement paralleling the highway was as overwrought as the track at the Penn Relays. Group after group of runners loped in either direction, chatting, keeping each other motivated, and working toward completing a long run penultimate to their appearance at the Honolulu Marathon, in the name of raising money for medical research.

Of course, what I was seeing is happening in cities all over the country, a massive and unforeseen revolution in the world of endurance sports. Millions of dollars pooled together for charities by people who, in many cases, are brand new to the marathons, bike centuries and triathlons they participate in. It's a super thing.

But one thing bothered me: too many of the runners had strapped elastic supports around their knees, and too many looked like they should probably be tackling a shorter distance before moving on to the marathon. In talks with coaches and participants over the past few years, I was disappointed to hear that many of the athletes-in-the-making are into it just long enough to finish the marathon or triathlon, and then they tend to return to their old ways. Here are a few thoughts harvested from those discussions, in the hopes that those putting in all the training and fundraising don't miss out on what many endurance athletes consider is the main point: making it a lifetime deal.

Getting into shape is one of the best things you can do for yourself. One barely has to look past the front page of the daily newspaper to get a report on the pitfalls of a sedentary lifestyle. The connection between obesity and diabetes — and a number of other diseases — has been proven by numbers that have been well crunched. Besides avoiding the associated medical dilemmas, being fit feels good, and a daily exercise fix becomes one of the favorite times of a reborn athlete's day, which leads us to the point.

Getting hooked on a daily workout is worth a million diet books. Here's the great secret that could put all the best-selling diet books out of business: Once you get past the initial alarm of working out and keep it up for long enough, exercise sessions go from being dreaded to being craved. And once you start craving a daily workout, the rest falls into place. You lose weight, you begin to covet broccoli and brown rice rather than drumsticks and Doritos, you sleep better, you feel better, and you burn off a typical day's stress rather than need to drown it at the bar.

Here are some tips to help you get hardwired into exercise

1. Start off doing less than you think you can. Your first objective is to develop confidence in your self-discipline. You're better off doing 20 minutes three times per week and gaining momentum than being overwhelmed by a schedule you're not ready to handle.

2. Start small and enjoy working your way up. After you get it going, enjoy the sense of accomplishment as you get stronger and become able to handle a heavier workload.

3. Incorporate strength training from the very beginning. Working with a coach or personal trainer, learn how to use weights properly and within the context of a smart program. Weight training and core body strength training — properly performed — are one of your best weapons against injuries, and a valuable tool to raising your performance in triathlon.

4. Commit to a minimum of a one-year program. The secret to getting hooked on consistent exercise: performance psychology expert Dr. Denis Waitley says to truly ingrain a positive habit, like an exercise discipline, a beginner needs not three weeks, not six weeks, but an entire year to do it. Anything less doesn't sink the claws in deep enough. While this is more a rule, and there are always exceptions, fully committing a year to an exercise discipline is a smart step toward making it a revolution to last a lifetime.

5. Make your first goal a training camp. Triathlon camps are possibly the best way to launch yourself into triathlon on the right road. From bike set-up to swim technique to walking away with a program tailored to your experience and desires, it's a fun way to hardwire yourself into the sport.

6. Hire a coach. Find a local tri club and ask about quality local coaching, or consider an online coach if no one is available. Then listen to them. There's no better way to establish and maintain solid progress than to work with a coach over the

long term. Coaches can evaluate your performance and figure your needs, as well as provide motivation and support. They also are keen to when you might be doing too much or are making a mistake that might trip you up with an injury.

7. Train with a group. Long runs and training rides become something to look forward to rather than workouts to be feared when you train with a group. It also pressures you to get out the door. Just be sure you hook up with athletes of similar ability, and beware groups that race in each and every workout. Training is training and racing is racing. Mixing the two is a common and injury-plagued error.

8. Connect yourself with the training ritual rather than obsessing about the goal. Many people get into triathlon with a single-minded goal, like finishing an Ironman or qualifying for the Hawaii Ironman. That's not enough of a payoff for all the work you're going to put in. Do it for the love of the training and satisfaction it brings. Racing is just the icing on the cake.

9. Make friends at the triathlon shop, the running shoe store, and the bike shop. Local running and bike shops are the conduits of the local athletic community. Go there for information and for recommendations about coaches and clubs, doctors and podiatrists. Get to know them and support them with your buying dollars, and they'll go out of their way to help you achieve your goals and enjoy the sport.

10. Measure your progress in detail. Keeping a daily training log and objectively measuring your fitness (body fat measurements, time trials, races, workout times, etc.) is a powerful tool in the production of training motivation and focus. Certain results come at such a slow pace that you might not notice them by sheer feeling. However, the cold numbers of measurement will serve as evidence to the benefits of your weekly toil.

2.2 Heart Rate Monitor 101

Almost every triathlon coach or triathlon program somehow or another has you watching your heart rate. It's the fundamental way a coach can make sure you're not overtraining, as pumped up beginners often do.

Ultimately, everyone using a heart-rate monitor to guide their training will be interested in a stress test or supervised time trial to figure their maximum heart rate. The following formula will give you a solid, useful start without any of the hassle or expense. And it works. Break out your monitor, grab a pencil, a calculator and notepad, and you're in business.

1.   Establish your Resting Heart Rate (RHR).

At a time when you haven't eaten for at least two hours, lay down and relax for 20 minutes with your heart rate monitor on. At the end of 20 minutes, check the reading on your watch for an instant picture of your Resting Heart Rate (RHR). The ideal time to do this is immediately after waking up in the morning. Testing your RHR on a daily basis and creating an average will help you refine your calculations.

2.   Establish your Predicted Maximum Heart Rate (PMHR).

You've heard of this one: simply subtract your age from 220 (this formula only works for adults). This is your PMHR.

3.   Establish your Heart Rate Reserve (HRR).

Subtract your RHR from your PMHR. This is your HRR.

4. Calculate training intensity percentages.

Now you're going to figure the target heart rate levels, which equate to percentages of your adjusted maximum heart rate.

0.50 x HRR + RHR = _____ (This is 50% of your maximum intensity effort)

0.60 x HRR + RHR = _____ (60%)

0.70 x HRR + RHR = _____ (70%)

0.80 x HRR + RHR = _____ (80%)

0.90 x HRR + RHR = _____ (90%)

5. These zones are specifically for your running. To calculate your cycling zones, subtract 10 beats from your PMHR and compute an additional set of scores. For swimming, subtract 15 beats from your PMHR and generate the set. Swimming is especially tricky to figure out because skill makes a huge difference, so be prepared to make adjustments at the pool.

6. The Zones

50-70% is the LSD (Long, Slow Distance) zone. It's where you want to be during your recovery workouts and your long over-distance efforts. Particularly with the long workouts, you'll improve efficiency and fat-burning abilities of your physiology. Long bike rides, long runs, easy spinning on the bike, light jogging, and easy laps in the pool are typical workouts associated with this zone.

70-80% is your Aerobic Capacity Zone. This is the higher range of your aerobic zone where you're really improving the cardiovascular plumbing of the body. This is the foundation of a triathlete's fitness. Usually, this should be limited to 60 minutes of exercise and lower, depending on your experience. Spending lots of time in both the LSD and Aerobic Capacity Zones is how you get good at triathlon.

80-90% *is your Anaerobic Zone. Training in the Anaerobic Zone should represent a relatively small fraction of a triathete's weekly training time, especially beginners, depending on your event and the time of year. Yet it's extremely effective for all, from sprint-distance specialists to the Ironman fanatic. This is usually the zone referred to when a tempo session or cruise interval session is called for.*

90% and above is your Max VO$_2$ Zone-the high-quality stuff of interval training. It's a domain that only the sprint-distance triathlete needs to worry about.

▲ **The Energy Efficient or Recovery Zone — 60% to 70%**
Training within this zone develops basic endurance and aerobic capacity. All easy recovery running should be completed at a maximum of 70%. Another advantage to running in this zone is that while you are happily fat burning, you may lose weight and you will be allowing your muscles to re-energize with glycogen, which has been expended during those faster-paced workouts. Check out the fat burning zone page.

▲ **The Aerobic Zone — 70% to 80%**
Training in this zone will develop your cardiovascular system. The body's ability to transport oxygen to, and carbon dioxide away from, the working muscles can be developed and improved. As you become fitter and stronger from training in this zone, it will be possible to run some of your long weekend runs at up to 75%, thus getting the benefits of some fat burning and improved aerobic capacity.

▲ The Anaerobic Zone — 80% to 90%

Training in this zone will develop your lactic acid system. In this zone, your individual anaerobic threshold is found — sometimes referred to as the point of deflection (POD). During these heart rates, the amount of fat being used as the main source of energy is greatly reduced and glycogen stored in the muscle is predominantly used. One of the by-products of burning this glycogen is the runner's worst enemy, lactic acid. There is a point at which the body can no longer remove the lactic acid from the working muscles quickly enough. This happens at an individual heart rate for us all and is accompanied by a rapid rise in heart rate and a slowing of your running pace. This is your anaerobic threshold or POD. Through the correct training, it is possible to delay the POD by being able to increase your ability to deal with the lactic acid for a longer period of time or by pushing the POD higher.

▲ The Red Line Zone — 90% to 100%

Training in this zone will only be possible for short periods of time. It effectively trains your fast-twitch muscle fibers and helps to develop speed. This zone is reserved for interval running and only the very fit are able to train effectively within this zone.

First, you need to know your Maximum Heart Rate (MHR). Be sure to get the all-clear from your doctor before attempting to find your MHR, as it requires an all-out effort. An easy way to do this is with an indoor trainer while wearing your heart rate monitor. Warm up by pedaling easily for 15-30 minutes. Now, increase resistance to a level that you can still pedal without jumping on the pedals. At 60-second intervals, increase either the gear or the resistance a notch. Continue until exhaustion. Record the highest heart rate you attain.

In a study published in a recent issue of *The Journal of the American College of Cardiology*, Dr. Seals and his colleagues devised a new formula: maximum heart rate equals 208 minus 0.7 times age. They used published studies involving 18,712 healthy people and data from 514 healthy people they recruited. Their formula gives much higher average maximum heart rates for older people, with the new and old heart rate curves starting to diverge at age 40.

((Max HR-Resting HR)*%X/100) + Resting HR.
(where %X = %MAX, e.g. 60)

The Karvonen Formula calculates your heart rate reserve range. To calculate it, take your pulse for one minute on three successive mornings upon waking. (We will be using the case of a 30-year-old male whose resting pulse was 69, 70 and 71 for an average of 70 over the three days.)

Calculate target heart rate by subtracting your age from 220 (220-30 = 190).

Subtract your average resting heart rate from target heart rate (190-70 = 120).

The lower boundary of the percentage range is 50% of this plus your resting heart rate [(120 x 0.5) + 70 = 130]. The higher boundary is 85% plus your RHR [(120 x 0.85) + 70 = 172]. Using the Karvonen Formula for percentage of heart rate reserve, this 30-year-old man should be working between 130 and 172 beats per minute (BPM).

How to Determine Your Heart Rate Training Range:

1. Heart Rate Reserve: The Karvonen Formula
▲ Find your Resting Heart Rate (RHR)
▲ Find your Predicted Maximal Heart Rate (HR max)
▲ HR max = 220-age
▲ Find your Heart Rate Reserve (HRR)
▲ HRR = HR max-RHR

Find the lower limit of your Heart Rate Training Range:

▲ Multiply your HRR by 50% and add your RHR
▲ HRR x 0.50 + RHR = Low Target Heart Rate

Find the upper limit of your Heart Rate Training Range:

▲ Multiply your HRR by 85% and add your RHR
▲ HRR x 0.85 + RHR = High Target Heart Rate

2. Percent of Heart Rate Max:
▲ Find your Predicted Maximum Heart Rate (HR max)
▲ HR max = 220-age

Find the lower limit of your Heart Rate Training Range

▲ Low Target Heart Rate = HR max X 0.50

Find the upper limit of your Heart Rate Training Range

▲ High Target Heart Rate = HR max X 0.90

2.3 Getting Your Weight Down Safely

If there's one fact that sports scientists, coaches and athletes agree on when it comes to a common trait in top athletes, it's this: a low body fat percentage. Citing the facts in hundreds of case studies, Dr. Michael Colgan, head of the Colgan Institute and one of the most highly regarded sports nutritionists in the world, is frank: "Body fat is dead weight."

To prove the point, Dr. Colgan, whose clientele have included the likes of Mark Allen, Dave Scott, Peter Reid and Lori Bowden, begins a session with a new client on the running track. "Yes, we've done this for a long time," Colgan says. "We have them sprint a full lap around the track at their best speed. We give them a chance to completely recover, and then we have them do it again with a 10-pound bodybelt around their waist." The dramatic effect, Colgan adds, reveals how much body fat erodes athletic performance.

"And that's just for the quarter-mile," he says. "For a triathlete out there for hour after hour, the effect is disastrous."

Optimum Range

The upshot of this message is the obvious truth: Those seeking a direct path to a substantial increase in performance are advised to strategically and accurately steer their body fat percentage into an optimum zone.

Ranges both safe and optimal for endurance athletes are as follows: Men 8-12 percent and women 10-15 percent.

Hazards of Popular Diets

After you've established that you want to burn off some dead weight, the first thing to do is clarify the common mistakes and pitfalls made by multitudes of athletes before you. Colgan has long said that "often athletes use methods that decimate both their performance and their health." Studies have shown time and time again that endurance athletes restricting their food intake nose-dive into a state of poor nutrition.

A study of women qualified for the Olympic Marathon trials showed that highly trained runners had low intakes of iron, zinc, copper, magnesium, calcium and overall calories. Colgan says that athletes subsisting on such diets are robbing themselves of the performance their weight-reducing diets are designed to achieve. The currently popular Atkins diet — recently condemned by the government -- funded Medical Research Council-may be one of the most visible examples of a fad diet that exacts harm.

"Atkins has fooled people into thinking it's the answer to life," says Colgan. "It's diets like these that are fatally flawed. They're designed to lose weight rather than correctly lose body fat. You lose it too fast, burn off muscle, and throw the body into a defensive state where it strives to preserve fat."

Doing It Right

In the three decades Dr. Colgan has been advising athletes, he's established a solid set of guidelines on correctly melting off the unwanted pounds. Below are several of the most essential rules he wrote about in *Optimum Sports Nutrition* and can be easily put into action by a triathlete in training.

1. **"Lose no more than half-a-pound of fat per week."**
   "Any weight loss of more than half-a-pound is a warning that you are reducing too much." Losing more, Colgan warns, alarms your body into retaining fat. By doing it gradually, you overhaul the "adipose cells, hormones, enzymes, capillaries and other tissues to suit."

2. **"Get your body fat measured every two months."** Do this to chart your progress and make sure you're losing fat, not muscle. Dr. Colgan champions the underwater weighing and infrared testing technologies offered at sports medicine clinics. Body fat calipers are less reliable, but oftentimes the most practical for many athletes.

3. **"Avoid all saturated fats."** Saturated fats have to be cut. Saturated fat calories hurdle their way past metabolic adjustments and sit themselves in adipose deposits.

4. **"Avoid all commercial diets."** You're wasting your time if you lose nutrients and muscle, as well as fat. You'll suffer athletically and probably put the fat right back on. Stay away from the fads.

5. **"No drugs or witches brew."** Those who ever popped an ephedra-based diet pill understand this one. Pills and lotions have wacky side effects and offer only temporary weight loss at best.

6. **"Cut the sugar; eat mainly complex carbs."** "I was running a marathon, and before and after I was seeing

guys eating six rolls or a big dessert, just destroying their insulin balance," recalls Dr. Colgan. Get a copy of the glycemic index of foods (easy to Google off the Web) and blanket your diet with low-glycemic carbs. High-glycemic carbs, as obvious as a can of Coke and not-so-obvious foods, such as a rice cake or bagel, induce an insulin spike that triggers the liver into converting the excess into fats.

7. **"Eat a high-fiber diet."** By eating 30-50 grams of fiber of day, you'll create a stable metabolism that favors using food as immediate fuel rather than stored fat. Oatmeal, cauliflower, beans and apples are good examples of fiber-rich foods.

8. **"Weight train to maintain lean muscle mass."** Weight training has the dual advantage of helping a triathlete prevent injury, while protecting or increasing an athlete's amount of lean muscle mass. The latter benefit is instrumental in burning up body fat and keeping it off for good.

9. **"Do low-intensity cardio work every day."** Obviously, this is the staple ingredient of the triathlon lifestyle. Doing so directly teaches your body how to efficiently burn fat as fuel.

10. **"Train in the mornings to boost your resting metabolic rate."** After a workout, Colgan says studies show the resting metabolic rate is boosted for as many as 18 hours. Training in the morning gives you the full effect of this, whereas training in the evening, the effects are trimmed once you hit the sack (RMR suffers a precipitous drop).

Advanced Techniques for Losing Body Fat

▲ **Maintain your Omega-3s and chromium levels.** In addition to the 10 methods listed above, Colgan advises athletes to maintain their Omega-3 fatty acid status, which helps your insulin metabolism. Such foods as fresh salmon and nuts are good sources of Omega-3s. He also recommends supplementing with 200-600 mcg chromium picolinate daily to keep your insulin metabolism in check.

▲ **Maintain your mitochondria.** Most recently, Dr. Colgan has been studying "excitotoxic brain dysfunction." Roughly defined as the breakdown of mitochondria by free radicals, Colgan says that between the ages of 26 and 60, there's a 50 percent natural decline in mitochondria function. The result is the feeling of fatigue, Colgan says, and when we feel tired like this, we often make the mistake of eating more. A key to healthy mitochondria is to supplement with acetyl-L-cartinine (500-2000 mcg per day) and R + alpha lipoic acid (100-800 mg per day).

▲ **Kick up your anabolic drive with doubles.** A natural for triathletes, by training two times per day, you'll burn body fat and increase lean muscle.

Fortunately for triathletes, the essential lifestyle alone is a great burner of body fat. But don't forget optimal nutrition strategies offered by certified experts, such as Dr. Colgan. You'll not only lose the pounds, you'll lose the *right* pounds.

Chapter 3

The Unbreakable Body

**INDISPENSIBLE ADVICE ON HOW TO PREVENT AND
DETER THE TRAINING-RELATED INJURY**

3.1 25 Commandments of Injury Prevention for the Triathlete

▲ **Get instruction.** Investing in a good coach or training camp and learning how to become a coachable athlete are the best two steps you can make toward an injury-free athletic career.

Good coaches know how to set up an intelligent schedule that incorporates necessary recovery time and yields smart progress. It also eliminates the stress of decision-making and planning that every self-coached athlete struggles with.

▲ **Use a heart-rate monitor.** Ideally, you'll learn to use a heart-rate monitor from your coach, as most triathlon coaches rely on the information spewed by the technology to effectively guide your training. The most valuable attribute of using a monitor is to keep you from going too hard. If you used a monitor to restrain yourself from leaping out of the aerobic zone your entire triathlon career, you'd be head and shoulders above most self-coached triathletes who go too hard and too often.

▲ **Develop a foundation of strength and balance.** Core strength, as it's popularly called, not only helps reduce the risk of injury due to imbalance and lack of support, but also helps you channel more power to locomotion. Balance is important in swimming, biking and running; muscular imbalances often lead into a downward spiral of performance, or at least lock us onto a plateau. Developing core strength and balance and keeping them in check are invaluable to a long and prosperous career. They're easy to find, too: Local fitness centers these days offer a variety of core classes: Pilates and athletic yoga. Books and videos are also easy to find. Talk with your coach about implementing a core program into your overall schedule.

▲ **Use uphill running for strength.** The greatest running coach of our times, Arthur Lydiard, says the key to preventing hamstring injuries (along with other running injuries) is to develop strength using hill training or running up stairs. It makes sense: running and bounding uphill is turned into strength work by virtue of gravity and bodyweight, and it's a much safer activity (and probably more effective) than doing heavy squats in the weight room. By adding a session or two of stair running or light hill repeats into your training week, you'll be in business.

▲ **Master technique.** In laying out a program, your coach will most likely give you drills to do for all three sports. Don't pass these up as unimportant. Drilling your technique will improve efficiency, enhance balance, improve specific flexibility and streamline the flow of power into speed.

▲ **Treat yourself to an occasional sports massage.** Over the last decade, some studies looking for the value of sports massage have come up empty. But it's almost impossible to find an elite endurance athlete these days who doesn't count on massage for enhanced recovery, relaxation, and injury prevention. If it's good enough for Lance Armstrong, it's good enough for you.

▲ **Don't overuse the track.** Track workouts are addictive because they give you specific feedback as to your fitness, and when you start getting stronger, stopwatch times plummet and you want to use the track more. But tracks are generally hard-surfaced and are always circular, both attributes that invoke injury danger, particularly when you're running fast. You can do speed and tempo workouts on the trail or on the road, and often to greater benefit. And most certainly lower the chance of getting hurt.

▲ **Don't run in broken-down shoes.** While the outsole on a pair of training shoes may not appear even remotely diminished (most are made of very tough carbon rubber), the true heart of a shoe is the midsole, which wears down much faster. Running shoes certainly aren't cheap, but if you can find a way to rotate in a fresh pair every three months (or sooner), you'll reduce the chance of certain types of injury.

▲ **Don't raise your running volume too quickly.** Bump your running mileage up too quick, and you can count on it bumping back. While your cardiovascular system responds rapidly to running, it takes the muscles, bones, tendons and ligaments some time to catch up. If you're new to running and triathlon, if you can make it through the first year by being patient in respect to volume increases (like increasing no more than 5-10% every three weeks), you'll have a solid, consistent year of base work under your belt. Getting injured because of impatience and being overly excited will waste most of it, and you'll be starting off right where you were at the beginning.

▲ **Incorporate mandatory rest days.** Taking one day off from training a week is a smart way to allow your body to recover, and also teaches your mind and body how to deal with a day without exercise. If you work a traditional Monday through Friday job and do a lot of training on the weekend, Mondays make a good pick for this technique.

▲ **Don't sacrifice sleep.** Only the occasional genetic freak can get away with training 20 hours a week or so for an Ironman while getting away with six or so hours of sleep. Most of us are going to need the full eight hours to fully recover (plenty of elite endurance athletes prefer 10-12 hours of sleep).

The key to remember is that progress is not made while you train; rather it's made while you recover. Skipping on sleep to get everything in is wasting your training time and effort, and the fun of it is going to evade you in a serious way.

▲ **Get your bike set up by an expert.** One of the best reasons to go to a good triathlon camp or to get a good triathlon coach is that one of the first things they do is check your bike set up.

Except for crashes, almost all cycling injuries can be traced to how a bike fits you, your position on the bike, and the type and setup of shoes and pedals. In addition to making sure your bike is set up, you can help it out by implementing core body strength training into your overall schedule.

▲ **Take glucosamine and chondroitin supplements for the knees.** The medical community is generally skeptical of these supplements that have been claimed by some to reduce knee pain and even repair cartilage. But as of right now, the scale seems tipped in support of glucosamine and chondroitin supplementation, and they appear to be safe to take. So if you're nearing or over the 40-year-old mark and have knee issues knocking on your door, this is a worthwhile investment. And of course, talk to your doctor about it.

▲ **Overwhelm early-warning injury signs with care.** Most injuries flash warning signs to let you know things are coming apart. Your job is to listen and act. San Francisco football great, Brent Jones, had a long career in the NFL because he attacked injuries with a fury, treating injuries diligently with ice, therapy and following any advice given to him by trainers as if it was divine guidance.

For example, let's say you finish a long run and in the last few miles you felt a tenderness arising within the Achilles tendon on your left foot.

Don't just dismiss it as something that will go away. Take immediate action with ice, elevation and evaluating what the cause of the problem is.

▲ **Treat your injury with ice, compression, elevation and rest.** But whatever you do, don't stretch it! When a tendon or muscle is pulsing with injury pain, resist the temptation to "stretch it out." At this point in time with an injury warning sign, the tissue is looking for a break from the action. Stretching is exactly the opposite you want to do at this time. It will just exacerbate the problem. Wait until the pain has gone away in a day or two (or more), and then gently re-introduce light stretching to the area.

▲ **Obey the request of a warning sign by taking a day off or switching to aerobic cross-training.** If a running injury has struck, along with aggressive first-aid, consider leaving the running shoes in the closet and spend a few days on your bike or in the swimming pool. The non-impact nature of swimming and biking will keep you fit and enhance dodging the injury with active recovery. During the cross-training days, continue to ice the site of the injury before and after your training.

▲ **Talk to an expert.** Many elite athletes have become elite because, in addition to addressing injury warning signs with first-aid and care, they immediately seek appropriate medical advice upon the flare up. Along with advanced treatment, a sports injury professional will help you map your way away from injury danger by recommending other forms of therapy like massage, and give you a set of specific instructions. Consult with the sports medicine world. Is there a leg length discrepancy? Are you making a technique mistake? Are you overtraining? Are your shoes right? By being aggressive in the beginning, you can dig injuries up by the root and kill them before they take hold.

▲ **Tell the medical expert you can only handle so much.** If a physical therapist or sports medicine expert writes up a therapy program that looks like it's going to take two hours a day, ask them if they can't pare it down a bit. Assuming you can still cross-train through an injury problem, if the program takes more than 30 minutes, there's a good chance you won't have the time or motivation to do it all. Sometimes less is more.

▲ **Decrease impact stress when healing.** We've already mentioned this, but it's worth mentioning again. While you're on the mend, and even when you're just being careful after getting an injury warning sign, take your running to a field of soft grass or trail. Stay off the pavement. Even better, buy a water-belt and do your run workouts in the pool. They're pretty boring, but the hydrotherapy action of the water will aid your therapy.

▲ **Use the Styrofoam cup trick.** This is a classic tool of many marathoners and ultrarunners: Take a Styrofoam coffee cup, fill it with water, and stick it in the freezer. After a workout, if you feel a bit of pain or tenderness on the knee or around the foot, take out your cup of ice, tear off the bottom, and rub it on the pain. By having a cup like this handy, it will increase the chances that you'll use it.

▲ **Take time off at the end of the season**. Training year in and year out will take its toll. Try and plan to take a month every year and have some fun with it, allowing your body to recover from the grind of running and triathlon. Play ping-pong, go hiking, or take up something different like rowing or aerobics. The mental break will be just as good for you as the physical break.

▲ **Recalibrate your head for a comeback.** If you've been away from the sport for a matter of months or years, then be sure to forget about how fast you were and train at the slower pace you need to. It might be frustrating and humiliating, but a comeback usually takes just as much time as it took to get to that amazing peak you used to be at. It's a humbling experience, but you have to let go or face punishment from the inevitable injury that awaits the impatient.

▲ **Cross-train your way down from being overweight.** Heaviness and running don't mix well. The impact stress delivered to the joints can be too much for a body struggling to adapt. Using triathlon to reduce your weight, get fit, and adapt to running gradually is one of the great benefits of multisport over pure running.

▲ **Remember that salt is your friend.** As a triathlete, you'll undoubtedly train or race in hot conditions. Heat injury is one of the most dangerous injuries you'll ever come close to. One of the reasons triathletes do get tripped by heat injury, particularly hyponatremia (when levels of sodium become dangerously low), is because they stick solely to water for fluid replenishment. Sports drinks, like Gatorade, have an appropriate amount of sodium within their mix, and not only replenish your sodium stores but help the body absorb water. In Ironman competitions, pretzels, soup, and other salty products may do well for you.

▲ **Study and apply good nutrition.** Over the long haul — and triathlon is a long haul — good nutrition will pay dividends in longevity and performance. The great triathletes, like Dave Scott, Paula Newby-Fraser and Mark Allen, will tell you face to face that nutrition was a critical component in their health and strength, year after year, victory after victory.

3.2 The Knees

It's a true story from the days of the running boom, and it goes like this: A top collegiate distance runner reported to his coach in emotional shambles. He'd start off on a training run and would be reduced to limping and then to a sorrowful walk. He was struck with severe knee pain, he told the coach. Sharp, mysterious and relentless.

The coach sent him off to an orthopedic specialist. Without a visual cue to work with (there was no swelling, for example), the doctor performed a surgical operation. Following the surgery were months of rehab to recover the atrophied muscles that had shrunk during the procedure. The runner finally got to put on his running shoes and test it out. The same exact pain in the same exact part of the knee fired up as if untouched by the surgery. He still couldn't run, and what followed was a repeat of the nightmare: another operation, months of therapy and with the exact same result: the pain resurfaced the moment he started to run.

Finally, the runner was referred to Dr. George Sheehan, the prototypical running doctor who eventually gained fame as a columnist for *Runner's World* and author of countless books. The first thing Dr. Sheehan asked the young distance star to do was take off his shoes so he could look at his feet. (The injured runner thought Sheehan was nuts. "I said my knee, not my foot.")

After a minute or so inspecting his patient's feet and shoes, he took scissors to a piece of cork, and inserted the cork underneath the insole of the shoe. He had the young man put his shoes back on and told him to go for a jog.

The pain was gone.

The moral of the story is that when a knee injury from running occurs, we first need to dismiss the common concept of athletic knee injuries that happen to football and basketball players. "It's awful rare that cartilage is going to be injured from running," says Dr. Keith Jeffers, a chiropractor, exercise physiologist and veteran runner based in San Diego. Dr. Jeffers, a.k.a. "The Running Doctor," says that knee injuries in football are likely caused by a leg getting twisted in a violent tackle. A runner's knee problem, on the contrary, is rooted in a biomechanical flaw flushed out by the thousands of footsteps a runner or triathlete takes every workout. The flaw, oddly enough, has little to do with the knee itself; the knee is simply the unlucky victim.

The two most common knee pains that result from distance running are Runner's Knee (peripatellar pain syndrome or medial patellar retinaculitis) and ilio-tibial band (ITB) friction syndrome. Symptoms of Runner's Knee include a localized pain underneath or near the kneecap that appears early in a run, or climbing and descending stairs. ITB friction syndrome symptoms include a sharp pain that appears on the outside of the knee. Many veteran triathletes, particularly of the half- and full-Ironman variety, will have experienced either one or both of these knee injuries at some point in their careers. Both are biomechanical flaws triggered most often by mistakes such as upping one's training mileage too drastically, too much racing, too much exposure to hard and cambered training roads, too much running on a track and footwear that's not doing the job.

▲ **Learning the hard way is no fun.** According to Dr. Jeffers, 25 percent of running injuries are of the knee pain variety. By following these tips, you will take valuable steps toward keeping yourself off the proverbial sideline.

▲ **Correct the mechanics of the foot with an insole.** "Research shows that 80-90 percent of runners have pronation problems," says Dr. Jeffers. Runner's Knee-type pains can often be solved-and prevented-with a simple correction to the runner's shoe. He adds that almost all of us can benefit from purchasing a generic over-the-counter-type foot orthotic, such as Superfeet, that adds a solid dose of arch support to a running shoe. "An orthotic also helps tract and stabilize the heel," he says. "When you tract the heel, you tract the knee." For those wanting to go the extra mile, consider visiting a recommended running doctor or podiatrist for an evaluation of foot mechanics and tendencies. A good place to get a recommendation of who to see is at a running shoe store or through your local triathlon community.

▲ **Massage the ilio-tibial bands.** The ilio-tibial band is a strip of fascia that originates in the hip and wraps down along the outside of the thigh, inserting itself into the shinbone below the knee. A massage therapist working on a non-runner can be pressed to find any sign of this band. But in a runner, the band is pronounced and taut. The general consensus as to the cause of ITB friction syndrome is that the leg is overwrought with the pounding, and gets so tight that it inflames the insertion of the band to a point of grinding pain. Too much running on hard surfaces, or running downhill, can contribute to this dilemma.

What's a good way to prevent this syndrome? Post-workout stretches are often recommended to loosen up the band, but Dr. Jeffer's warns that this can do more harm than good. "The best way to stretch the ilio-tibial band is through massage," he says. Rather than yanking on the ends

of the band with a stretch, an action that can mess you up with micro-tears, spreading out the band with massage techniques lengthens the band safely. Seeing a professional sports massage therapist once every week or two is the best way to do this, but you can also harvest benefits by having a partner press and massage along the band. Rolling your bodyweight along the band on foam rollers (easy to find in the modern-day fitness center) is another inexpensive way to self-massage the band.

▲ **Strengthen the hamstrings.** "Many people think it's the quadriceps that stabilize the knee, and they weight train these muscles to prevent knee injuries," says Dr. Jeffers. But don't forget the hamstrings, he warns. "It's the hamstrings that actually do more work to stabilize the knee." He recommends the following exercise: On your knees, either hook your heels underneath a couch, or have partner hold them down for you. Keeping your back straight, lean forward as much as you can, slowly, and return to the vertical starting position. Repeat. As your hamstrings grow stronger, you'll be able to lean farther and farther forward. Along with helping you to prevent knee injuries, this exercise can help beef up the upper part of your hamstrings, another spot vulnerable to injury.

▲ **Correct your strength imbalances.** Along with correcting the biomechanics of the feet, analyzing and correcting the various imbalances surrounding your core muscle groups (abdominal, hips, back muscles) and the legs is vital. Consider getting a full-scale evaluation at a sports medicine clinic or from a running doctor to gain awareness of your weak points. They'll usually prescribe specific exercises to get you back in balance. Exercise techniques, such as Pilates and core conditioning classes, are also appropriately useful for triathletes.

▲ **Seek out smart running surfaces.** If possible, run on trails for at least 50 percent of your run training. Avoid running on tracks except for interval sessions. When running on the road, beware of cambered surfaces — use flat, even roads and sidewalks when possible. Long, brutal downhills are to be avoided as well.

▲ **Obey the slightest warning sign.** We mentioned feelings of invincibility. What this usually leads to is egotistically thinking you can run through any pain tossed your way. Wrong answer. The best response to the slightest tinge of discomfort you can describe as *musculoskeletal* is to break out the ice bag and immediately get an evaluation as to what might be going on. Do you need new running shoes? Have you been stretching and strengthening? Do you need to lower your mileage? Immediate precautions include icing for 10 minutes before and after a run, and consider focusing your training on biking and swimming for a few days.

Responding to the body's signals with this kind of ferocity, and using all the preventative tips mentioned, will help you make strides toward a more true invincibility.

3.3 The Chronic Muscle Tear

How to Treat the Injury that Drives Runners and Triathletes Crazy

"The chronic muscle tear is probably the third most common injury among all groups of runner," writes Dr. Timothy Noakes, the quintessential runner/doctor in his encyclopedic work *The Lore of Running*.

I came across these words in my own frantic quest for an answer to a hamstring injury that had plagued me for nine months. The words that leaped up at me from off the page were the following:

"Chronic muscle tears are usually misdiagnosed, can be very debilitating and will respond to only one kind of treatment. The characteristic feature is the gradual onset of pain, in contrast to the acute muscle tears dramatically sudden onset of pain." This characteristic matched my problem exactly.

"In contrast to bone or tendon injuries, both of which improve with sufficient rest, chronic muscle tears will never improve unless the correct treatment is prescribed."

Noakes' book rang another bell for me here, as I had tried taking days off, and later weeks with no running, only to lace up my shoes, hit the road and feel as if, in terms of my injury, an hour hadn't passed. Noakes goes on to say that he was witness to one runner who had struggled with a chronic tear for five years.

Noakes advises that you can identify a chronic tear with the help of a physiotherapist, having him or her plunge two fingers deep into the location of the pain and search for a hard and tender knot. Noakes states that if a knot is found, then you're dealing with a chronic tear. In my case, the knot was very easy to find, deep in the belly of the left hamstring and hard as a marble.

Noakes believes that, while the mechanism behind a chronic tear is unknown at this point, specific sites on the body that digest large amounts of pounding (from running mileage), overuse (an endurance-sport given) and high-intensity loads (from speed or power training) are the areas most likely to sustain this type of injury.

Noakes observed that chronic tears tend to show their ugliness when an athlete makes an increase in mileage and/or intensity. In my case, I could jog around forever without much problem, but when I tried to run at any speed faster than a seven-minute pace, I found myself rapidly reduced to an infuriating limp.

"Conventional treatment, including drugs and cortisone injections, is a waste of time in this injury," writes Noakes, and he goes on to illustrate the technique he deems effective: cross-friction muscle massage, a physiotherapeutic technique detailed in the 10th edition of the British *Textbook of Orthopedic Medicine.*

The maneuvers are applied directly to the injury site, perpendicular to the injured muscle, and must be applied vigorously. "If the cross-friction treatment does not reduce the athlete to tears, either the diagnosis is wrong and should be reconsidered or the physiotherapist is being too kind."

Five to 10 five-minute sessions of cross-friction should correct the problem, says Noakes, but more may be necessary depending on how long the athlete has had the injury.

Runner's World's Dr. George Sheehan had once forwarded a desperate letter to Noakes from a runner who had tried everything to overcome a chronic muscle tear, having suffered from the tear for more than a year. Noakes wrote to the runner, advising him of the cross-friction techniques. He also suggested that he stay away from static stretching exercises, as it would only exacerbate the problem until it was sufficiently healed.

As I mentioned, when I found the Noakes material, I had made no progress whatsoever in getting effective treatment. Within a week of cross-frictions and no stretching, I observed a substantial and positive change in the strength within my hamstring. A month later, I was able to perform speed workouts again without deteriorating into a limp.

Once a chronic muscle tear has been tamed, an athlete should work aggressively to prevent a recurrence of the problem.

Incorporate a quality weight-training program into your training schedule, include moderate amounts of stretching. Upon noticing the first hint of reinjury, immediately apply more cross-frictions.

"A little treatment early on in these injuries saves a great deal of agony later," Noakes says.

3.4 Taking to the Trails

As mentioned earlier, one of the best ways you can make strides in the injury-prevention business is to do a steady proportion of your running on trails. The lower impact stress and the variety of terrain not only helps prevent injury, but gives you an enhanced training effect. Trails are also one of the most addicitive places to run. Scenic beauty, peacefulness, and fresh air.

One of the true contemporary masters of the trail is Scott Jurek. In 2004, Jurek captured his sixth consecutive Western States 100-mile ultramarathon, considered by many to be the most competitive and difficult trail race in the world. Below are Scott's recommendations for how to get the most out of the off-road run.

Scott Jurek's Guide to Hitting the Long-Distance Trail

1. **Recovery.** To do well in long distance trail running, you have to train consistently, which means you need to avoid getting sick and hurt. Don't spend all your training time running. Jurek stretches every day, gets plenty of sleep, gets massages and eats well.

2. **Be consistent.** You can't expect to run to your ability if you only train on the weekends. Putting in mileage during the week, year round, is the way to harvest your deeper talents.

3. **Use good form.** Learn and practice good running technique. Coaching can help you here, as well as flexibility work, Tai Chi, and simply paying attention.

4. **The effect.** "Trail running is a form of cross-training itself," Jurek says. The softer surface and the varied terrain work plenty of muscle groups without the typical damage done by long miles on the roads.

5. **Tune in.** Enjoy the scenery, but don't forget to watch where you're going, drink plenty of fluids and take in enough calories.

6. **Eat well.** Jurek says most athletes aren't getting enough nutrients in their diets, not to mention calories. He recommends the book, *Becoming Vegan* by Vesanto Melina for those interested in following his nutritional footsteps.

7. **Speed work.** Long, slow distance builds the engine, but speed work modifies the stock car into a race car. Fartlek on the trails is a good choice.

8. **Hill work.** Jurek does repeats on long hills, practicing not just tough ascents, but well-paced descents. The work builds strength and prepares the muscles for the pounding.

3.5 Building Core Strength for Multisport

Canadian Donna Phelan is a professional Ironman triathlete and certified personal trainer based in Encinitas, California.

Written and designed exclusively for this book, we asked Donna to develop an accessible core fitness program for the new triathlete or the veteran triathlete new to this brand of training (some the most hard-bodied triathletes will fail completely with certain simple tests of core strength and core balance, a condition that leaves them vulnerable to injury and power drain).

The following is Donna's prescription:

The core is one of the most important sources of physical strength, but one of the most neglected areas by triathletes. The centralized "core" area is the center of the body and the beginning point for movement. It refers to the lumbar-pelvic-hip complex, a pillar between the upper body and lower body.

A weak core leads to inefficient movement and predictable patterns of injury. That weakness causes undue stress on peripheral muscles of the upper extremity and lower extremity.

A core stability program will help you gain strength and a greater biomechanical advantage for swimming, biking and running. The following are some basic core exercises that will benefit triathletes. With each of these exercises, they should be performed comfortably and pain-free.

A. The Plank

Begin by lying face-down on the floor with feet together and forearms on the ground, shoulder width apart (Picture 1).

Draw the abdominals inward, squeeze your glutes and lift your entire body off the ground, forming a straight line from head to toe — envision your body as a plank of wood. Hold for a length of time that is challenging but comfortable. Begin with two sets, advancing to as many as five to 10 sets.

When you've mastered the plank, the next step is to add hip extension (Picture 2). Begin by performing the plank, then extending one hip at a time by activating the glutes and lifting your leg three to four inches off the ground. Hold for five to 10 seconds, then slowly return the starting position and repeat with the opposite leg.

B. Glute Bridge

This exercise helps develop muscle recruitment and firing of the glutes. Start by lying on your back, with your knees bent at 90 degrees and feet flat on the floor (Picture 3).

Contract your glutes and raise your hips toward the ceiling, forming a straight line between your hips and shoulders. The only point of contact with the ground should be your feet, shoulders and head. Maintain a strong glute contraction and hold for 10 seconds. Lower your hips to the floor and repeat three to five times.

An advancement of this exercise is to add "marching," one leg at a time (Picture 4). Simply raise one bent knee while in the bridge position and hold for three to five seconds. Alternate legs and repeat three to five times.

Picture 3

Picture 4

C. Opposing Arm and Leg Raises

Begin on all fours with your abs drawn in and your chin tucked toward your chest (Picture 5).

Slowly raise one arm (with your thumb pointing up) and at the same time lift the opposite leg.

Keep both your arm and leg straight while lifting them to body height. Hold for five to 10 seconds, and return your arm and leg to the ground.

Repeat with the opposite arm and leg, and perform three to five repetitions.

Picture 5

D. Hip Crossover

The objective of this exercise is to build mobility and strength in your torso by eliminating the use of your hips and shoulders.

Begin by lying on your back, arms extended out at your sides, knees bent and feet flat on the floor. Raise your lower legs to a 90-degree hip position (Picture 6) and slowly lower them to one side until they reach the floor (Picture 7). Raise them again to the starting position and lower them to the opposite side (Picture 8).

Remember to keep your abs drawn in and your torso and shoulders in contact with the ground. Begin with five repetitions to each side.

E. Ball Crunch

This is a variation of the standard crunch done on a flat surface. For this exercise you will need a stability ball.

Begin by lying on your back, arms folded across your chest (Picture 9). Be sure your knees are bent at a 90-degree angle and feet are flat on the floor, toes pointing straight ahead.

Draw your abs in and slowly crunch your upper body forward, raising your shoulders off the ball, and chin tucked toward your chest (Picture 10).

Hold for two to three seconds, then return to the starting position. Repeat five to 10 times.

For more information on Donna's training, go to her website at www.ipushfitness.com.

3.6 Generating a Foundation of Health

Formerly a national-class pole vaulter AND sub-2:30 marathoner, Ken Grace is a top California-based track coach, who has worked with everyone from the junior college distance runner to national-class marathoners and triathletes.

A longtime student of kinesiology and exercise science, Ken loves pushing the envelope of applying fresh research to helping his athletes perform at their best, and to stay healthy doing it.

In the following chapter, Ken boils down some of the principles he holds essential for achieving and maintaining athletic excellence and health.

Principles to Follow If You Want to Improve Your Physical Performance and Your Well Being

1. Eat Breakfast. Start your morning with a 12-ounce glass of water. Then eat a nutritious breakfast that includes a piece of fruit, protein, low-glycemic carbohydrates and a multivitamin/mineral supplement.

A tablespoon of flaxseed oil, or two tablespoons of ground flaxseed mixed with juice, helps to supply the essential fats (Omega 3 and Omega 6) in the proper proportions.

People who eat breakfast on a regular basis have a higher lean mass and feel better throughout the day.

The multivitamin/mineral should contain the following:

Vitamin C	1000 mg
Beta-Carotene	10,000
Vitamin E (D-alpha-tocopheryl)	800 IU
Selenium	200 mcg
Iron (Women may need more)	15 mg
Zinc picolinate	15 mg
Chromium picolinate	200 mcg
Folic Acid	400 mcg
CoQ 10	30 mg
Copper	0.5 mg
B2, riboflavin	10 mg
B3, niacin	25 mg
B6, pyridoxine	15 mg
B12, cyanocobalamin	25 mcg
Magnesium*	400 mcg
Potassium	500 mg
Calcium*	1000 mg*

Calcium and magnesium should be taken in a 2 to 1 ratio. A calcium/magnesium tablet usually is taken along with a multivitamin/mineral supplement because of the size of the tablet.

2. Try to Eat 5 or 6 Small Meals Each Day. The goal is to keep your blood sugar constant throughout the day. This is accomplished by eating something every two hours or so. After a good breakfast have a snack at around 10 am that includes fruit, a low glycemic carbohydrate and water. People, who eat lots of small meals keep their blood sugar level constant without any big highs or lows. In the long run, a consistent blood sugar, combined with a good exercise program, leads to fat loss and a growth of lean mass. Use your snack time to increase your fruit and vegetable intake for the day. Five meals a day would be: Breakfast, a morning snack, Lunch, afternoon snack & Dinner. If you have a snack after dinner try to make it a high protein/low fat snack before 8 pm.

3. Drink 8 to 10 Glasses of Water Daily. Water is the medium for every chemical reaction in the body. When you are dehydrated your body does not adapt and improve efficiently. In addition to drinking water, we are supposed to get a great majority of our water through a high daily intake of fruits and vegetables. Our natural mineral and vitamin demands are supposed to be met through the intake of fruits, nuts and vegetables.

4. Don't Spike Your Insulin. This is done by eating foods that are low in Glycemic Index and eating lots of small meals. Avoid high glycemic foods like French fries, sodas and simple sugars.

5. There are No Quick Fixes. Once you start a sound nutrition program...stick with it. It takes time to grow things right! It takes a good 3 to 6 months for all your cells to adapt and grow stronger. A red blood cell lives for 90 days before it is replaced. Make sure the protein you eat is sufficient first class protein and not a burger and fries!

A whey protein isolate drink is something to consider. Fish that live in cold water like Salmon, Tuna or Mackerel are excellent sources of protein. You need a protein source that is low in saturated fat!

6. Take Essential Fats Daily. Omega 3 and Omega 6 oils are essential to good health. Your cells need these fats on a daily basis for cellular metabolism. Flaxseed oil, olive oil and fish oils are examples of good fats. A daily tablespoon of flaxseed oil meets this need.

7. Avoid Partially Hydrogenated Oils and Saturated Fats. These are not good for your health. And they are definitely not essential fats. They are hard for your cells to metabolize. Saturated fats and partially hydrogenated oils are solid at room temperature. The essential fats are liquid.

8. Avoid Eating Chemicals Made by Man. Avoid eating or drinking food that contains Aluminum. Aluminum is a man made alloy that has no purpose being in the body. Recent studies suggest that excess aluminum in the body causes a number of disorders. Avoid drinks or foods that come packaged in aluminum. Check your deodorant and toothpaste. Try to eat foods that are in natural state and unprocessed. Remember good food spoils quickly. If it has a long shelf life...BEWARE!

9. Be Active. Do something active everyday. This could be as simple as a 20 minute walk, or run, at 70% of your maximum heart rate or a 40 minute weight training routine. The key is to move daily on a consistent basis.

10. Eat Lots of Vegetables and Fruit. The U.S. Government says five servings per day. Ancient man ate more like 10 servings per day... and we are direct descendants. Our fiber intake, along with minerals and vitamins, comes mainly through fruits, nuts and vegetables. We need 30 to 50 grams of fiber daily.

11. Stretch and Relax Everyday. Take time to do some stretching everyday to lengthen your muscles and relieve tension. Hold each stretch for 30 to 60 seconds and do not bounce. Finish with 10 to 20 minutes of relaxation, focusing on your breathing.

For more training suggestions from Ken, visit his website at www.coachkengrace.com.

PART II
THE UNBREAKABLE SPIRIT

Chapter 4

No Denial

STORIES OF AGE-GROUP TRIATHLETES BREAKING DOWN WALLS

4.1 Marian Davidson's Impossible Comeback

At the 2002 Vineman triathlon, 61-year-old Marian Davidson raced with a fanny-pack on. Just in case, the fanny-pack contained a check that she could make out and hand over if she qualified for the Hawaii Ironman.

At any given qualifier, many triathletes show up and begin the race without strong expectations of winning a Hawaii slot, but everyone knows that on race day, anything goes. We see the variables at work all the time: who shows up, who's hot, who's not. Then the award ceremony comes up, and the slot gets passed up by those who have already qualified and those who don't want it. The drama of who finally gets the golden tickets to Hawaii can be as dramatic as the race itself.

In the story of Marian Davidson of Portola Valley, Calif., the drama leading up to the post-race moment she dipped happily into her fanny-pack goes back much farther than the 7 hours and 6 minutes it took her to finish second in the 60-64 age group. Drama is the correct word. Despite growing up in a time when opportunities for women, athletic and otherwise, existed well outside the margin, she still got into Yale medical school and embarked on a career as an emergency room physician. These past two years, she has spent fighting through a minefield of bad luck just to get to the starting line of Vineman, and her path to Hawaii goes into the books as one of the classic tales that the Ironman tends to conjure.

Despite the complications of degenerative arthritis, Davidson decided to become a triathlete in 1998, after she volunteered to help out in the medical tent of the Hawaii Ironman. "I was inspired by everything I saw," she recounts. "I decided to give the sport a try. What did I have to lose?"

The following spring, she entered the mountain biking sprint triathlon at Wildflower. "I was terrified," she says. "I'm not an athlete; I never have been an athlete. But I did it! I did it, even though I was barcly able to run."

Shortly thereafter, Davidson, who lives with her husband and fellow triathlete, Michael, began working under the tutelage of triathlon coach Marc Evans. Evans has been coaching triathletes for two decades and is known throughout the sport as the first-ever triathlon-specific coach.

Despite the long history of coaching, Evans is as cutting-edge as they come. His approach spans from the larger-scale needs of aerobic and power development to the microscopic details of technique, using every tool he finds worthy. But Davidson's affection for her coach goes well beyond his technological wizardry:

Evans, who is only interested in working in one-on-one coaching relationships, is the antithesis of a Web-based computer coach. The two remain in constant communication, they meet for workouts and testing sessions, and a similar sense of humor binds them. "He's a bit weird and a bit crazy," says Davidson. "That's one of the reasons I like him so much."

By her own account, Davidson is not an easy project to take on. "I can't swim," she remarks. "I had only piddled around on a bike. And I can't run either." But one thing she can do is execute a plan.

"If I'm told to do something, I do it. I'm very Type A," she admits. Her training log itself serves as heavy evidence: an extra not required by Evans — she took it on herself — resembles the lab book of an electrical engineer working on a skyscraper.

Every workout is meticulously recorded in color-coded detail, including the riding work she does on her beloved show horse, Patrick. Riding in shows is the other sport Davidson took up in her 50s.

"The Year of Hell"

It was such precision and self-discipline that allowed her to persevere through the months leading up to Vineman.

"It was the year of hell," Davidson says with a sigh. In the last weeks of training before the June 2001 San Jose International triathlon, a goal race for her, the first of three freak disasters occurred. She was at her horse's side when, while talking with a friend, the friend revealed that she was battling cancer. "I was shaken up by the news, and I startled Patrick."

When Patrick "freaked out," the fingertips of four of Marian's fingers, looped in the reins, were torn off from her right hand. Three were surgically re-attached, but the middle fingertip couldn't be saved.

Davidson recovered in time to compete in the Pacific Grove triathlon in September, where she won her first age-group championship in an Olympic-distance event. Two weeks later, competing in a horse show, she was thrown from her horse and landed badly, directly on her head.

"When I hit the ground, I thought I was going to die," she says. While she didn't die, Marian did suffer broken vertebrae and a central spinal cord contusion. It turned out, remarkably, to be something she would eventually heal from.

"The paramedics who came all knew me from when I worked at the Stanford University Hospital," Davidson says. "It was like 'old home' week."

After the injuries were healed, Davidson began preparing for the Wildflower triathlon in May. On a training trip to Lake San Antonio in early April, Davidson suffered a third accident that would prove — despite first appearances — to be the scrape that would come closest to being fatal.

While riding her bike over a section of gravel road, her glasses fell down to the bridge of her nose, and in the moment she pushed them back up, things got awkward. She crashed to the ground.

"It left me with some deep abrasions, but I was still able to finish the ride." It was a week after the accident that the real trouble began.

"Six days after the crash, I was shaking with the chills." It had turned out that Davidson, who is allergic to antibiotics, had developed a severe case of cellulitis, a deep infection of the skin and tissues below the skin. For two weeks, she remained hospitalized and hooked up to IVs, coming dangerously close to dying. A small woman, her weight had dropped from 112 pounds to 106.

But, once again, she bounced back. Her greatly relieved husband quipped, "It's never boring around you."

And her desire to race a half-Ironman was fully intact. Both she and Michael decided to do the Vineman in early August.

Strange how persistence pays off: Both Marian and Michael would have great races in the wine country of Northern California.

When she called Evans, who also coaches Michael, to tell him the news of her qualification for the Hawaii Ironman, it was the completeness of the day that struck the coach emotionally. Michael, who trains around a schedule challenged by his law career and a daily two-hour commute, recorded a breakthrough split on the bike leg of Vineman.

Evans said the report brought him to tears. "It wasn't just all the adversity that they had been through, but that the two of them had their best race performances on the same day. That really made it special for me."

"If you grade their performances on a curve that takes into account their age and their careers," Evans continues with pride, "what they achieved were world-class performances."

"On those rides, I went out and bonked on purpose," he

4.2 Chris Sustala's Battle with the Bulge

Christopher Sustala had been an athlete all his life. It seemed a given. Yet, when the Texas A&M engineering student was a semester away from graduating, the variables would begin to change, and his body would snowball the other direction.

For years, Sustala had been taking on some of the more grueling events in competitive swimming for Texas A&M, including arduous monsters like the 200 fly and the 400 IM. At the time, he was a powerfully fit 190 pounds. "What happened was my athletic eligibility ran out when I still had that last semester of academic work to do," recalls Sustala, who is now 32 and lives in the Houston area. "So I started doing some coaching for the team. Which meant that even while I didn't have to swim anymore, I still got to eat in the athlete's dorm." The food doesn't only taste better in the athlete's cafeteria, reports Sustala, but it's all-you-can-eat.

The voracious appetite that fought to put back the calories he burned during swimming was still in full operation, as if by momentum. But Sustala's work at the pool was now all from the deck, and the calories mounted up in oversupply. He began to put on pounds.

He took his first job as a mechanical engineer. With focus now on work, he was oblivious to the dietary missteps he was accruing in his routine. "Generally, I'd skip breakfast. If I got hungry at the office, there were usually donuts and the like around. I wouldn't eat lunch until halfway through the day. And at night, I'd eat a big dinner."

The pattern took shape and time took its toll. Sustala's weight climbed upward into husky elevations. His scale began to read 300 pounds and over. Alarm grew.

"What really got my attention was that I started waking up at 2 a.m. with heartburn," Sustala recalls. This was about six years ago. "I knew something had to be done. My brother, Tommy, and a friend, Kevin, were doing triathlons and proposed a challenge. My triathlon career began."

For starters, Sustala's greatest "challenge within the challenge" was running, and his first precarious steps were taken in 100-yard gulps, with 200-yard walks in between. But he was steadfast in his pursuit, and he improved enough to enter a triathlon.

"I successfully completed an Olympic distance triathlon and was hooked," he says. "I then set two goals. One was to lose weight and the other became to do an Ironman. It might never happen, but I would have to train for it in case it ever did."

Sustala realized that if he were ever to take on an Ironman, he first had to tackle a marathon. He had burned his weight down to 250 for his first attempt of the 1998 Houston Marathon.

His goal was to break 4 hours, mighty ambitious considering his weight, but understandable considering his athletic background and the mindset that comes with it. Sustala finished in 4:50, and, although disappointed he'd missed his time goal by almost an hour, he did finish.

He tried again the following year under a particularly blazing Texas sun, but dropped out at mile 23 from dehydration. "In 1999, I had Achilles tendonitis. And then, in 2000, I finally broke 4 hours with a 3:53. Meanwhile, I'd been racking up experience in the local sprint, Olympic distance and even a half Ironman."

2002 would prove to be a pivotal year, as Sustala lowered his marathon PR to 3:33 and his weight to 230. Earlier in the year, at 205 pounds, he raced to an amazing 3:09 finish and qualified for the Boston Marathon.

"But Boston had never been my goal," he says. "My goal had always been the Hawaii Ironman. So I decided to enter the lottery." As if a mystical reward for his commitment to regaining his fitness, his entry into the Ironman Lottery — his first — was a success. In training for the event that followed the next month, Sustala had shed off another 15 pounds. He was now at his college race weight of 190.

Sustala's work as a mechanical engineer now involves specializing in chemical and waste treatment plants. Weekdays he works 8 to 5. His training exists outside of these borders, either early morning or early evening. He travels often, mostly to Michigan and Georgia, work trips he deals with the best he can in regard to his training. "I've done my share of runs in mall parking lots," he says.

Throughout this adventure, Sustala repeatedly credits his wife, Shelby — who is also a mechanical engineer — with his fitness turnaround. "She's been so amazingly supportive. She does the same kind of work I do. We actually met in college, so she knew me when I wasn't fat. But I think she's about at her limit now. After this is over, it will be time to become a husband again."

"She's started to ask why I can't apply myself to helping clean the house the way I apply myself in my training. She asks me, 'Why don't you pretend it's a race?'"

Chris Sustala successfully went on to finish the 2003 Hawaii Ironman. It was an opportunity he didn't take lightly. Said Sustala before beginning the race, "This is a once in a lifetime experience. It's happening much sooner than I had planned." In Sustala's case this turned out to not be a bad thing at all.

Chapter 5

No Excuses

THE IRONMAN AS A SELF-TEST

5.1 The Attraction of the Hawaii Ironman

"People are too durable, that's their main trouble. They can do too much to themselves, they last too long."
— Bertolt Brecht

Dave Parramore, a major in the U.S. Army, remembers a day when he was commanding a Black Hawk helicopter in Honduras. Fierce storms started mudslide disasters in Venezuela, and Parramore's unit was dispatched to help.

"We had to pass through six South and Central American countries," Parramore says. "There was no visibility. At one point, winds had blown us 150 miles off-course. We made it, but that was a day we later joked about how we set a record, three times, of 'almost' getting killed."

Parramore flew Black Hawks for 10 years, so you have to figure he's a guy with a titanium stomach. Yet, it was landing at Keahole Airport last October, with a Hawaii Ironman lottery slot, that gave the officer jitters.

"As the wheels touched down in Kona, beginning my arrival at the site of the Ironman Triathlon World Championship," he says matter-of-factly, "I felt like throwing up."

This is where we begin to discuss why the Hawaii Ironman is the most grueling triathlon. Going on 26-years-old, the legacy and power of the original long-distance triathlon continues to wreak havoc on all who come to test her. Part of the misery it evokes is due to the fear and awe Hawaii commands. In 1993, a rookie pro named Peter Reid arrived for his first attempt. Reid was excited not only to race, but to drink in the race-week atmosphere. "I did it all," he admits. "I swam from the pier everyday. I biked on the Queen K. I ran on Ali'i Drive. I hung out in the expo. I couldn't get enough of it." Comparison with competitors was impossible to restrain. "I had trained really, really hard," he says. "But in Kona I felt like the fattest guy on the island." The Canadian — who has since won the race three times — was smoked by mile 35 of the bike. He DNF'd.

Although you can design courses that, on paper, appear more challenging than Hawaii (Ironman Lanzarote is one of them), the pre-race prologue in Hawaii uniquely saps an athlete's strength. Some 1,600 triathletes, peaked and ripped after months of hard training, overwhelm the Kona village with sinewy muscles and fraying nerves. It's forgotten that Hawaii is a premium tourist spot. "At other Ironmans, race week is mellow. At Hawaii, everyone has their game face on," says long distance specialist, Beth Zinkand, who broke into the top five in 2000. Zinkand first raced Hawaii in 1996. "It's a nerve-wracking atmosphere. Everybody's looking each other over, trying to figure out who is going to beat who. Then your mind works against you. You start stressing about your training. 'Am I running enough miles? Should I have worked out more on the bike?'"

Dr. Joann Dalkoetter, who finished second in the 1982 Hawaii Ironman, is a sports psychologist and author of the book *Your Performance Edge*. She says that if you're unprepared, the countdown to a big event can burn you out beforehand. "Athletes get caught up not just with comparing bodies, but with everything else. You can be awed by your competitors' bikes, or the way they trained for the race. You wonder if you have the right equipment; the right nutritional supplements." Fear affects the physiology, she warns. "The stress response releases hormones into the body. Adrenaline; epinephrine. Blood pressure rises. You get a headache. You can't sleep because you're worried, and then you worry about the worrying."

Clinical psychologist and consultant for the Oakland Raiders, Paul Guillory, says the stress drains your energy stores. "At the beginning of a race, it's good to be pumped up. But you don't want to get caught up in days of self-criticism and panic," he says. "Anxiety really wears you out."

"It's such a high-strung environment," Reid explains. "You can never relax."

The stress can cause lack of hunger and constipation. Skittish athletes pack race bags and transition kits, terrified of misplacing shoes and salt tablets. Arriving three or four days early is an inadequate exposure for the triathlete struggling to adapt to the humidity, producing an overly elevated heart rate during taper jogs and spins. Some lose it and launch into Kamikaze workouts. By the time the sun begins to rise on race morning, you're chemically fried.

Race morning brings fresh terror. The Kailua Bay, tranquil-looking and sapphire blue, resembles a shark tank thanks to the hostility of a mass swim start. "Nothing compares to Hawaii," Zinkand says. "I'm fine swimming in most Ironmans, but Hawaii's brutal. The age-group men thrash you. I've had moments where I wondered if I could go on. It's as if you're supposed to have a water polo background."

"The water has it in for you," Reid adds. "It's tougher than it looks. You don't have a wetsuit, and the currents and eddies are deceptively strong."

After the swim there is a 112-mile bike leg with winds blowing against you at 30 to 40 miles per hour. In the final miles to the Hawi turnaround, gusts have been reported at over 60 miles per hour. Cyclists have been blown off their bikes. The same winds have an annoying knack for reversing directions to slow the ride back. Sun and humidity then punish the marathoners.

If you DNF in Hawaii, you're in good company. Reid started off with DNFs in 1993 and 1994. In his rookie year, in 1981, Scott Molina suffered heat exhaustion and quit. Julie Moss dropped out of the 1985 Hawaii Ironman with severe abdominal cramps. Erin Baker dropped out in 1986.

Mark Allen packed it up in 1982 when his derailleur broke. In 1987, he lost his lead to Dave Scott with four miles to go. While he refrained from stopping, his second-place finish came with internal bleeding.

Peril strikes even the masters. Reid followed his fourth-place breakthrough in 1997 with first in 1998, second in 1999 and first in 2000. It looked like he had the race by the throat. In 2001, hobbled by over-training, Reid DNF'd. Under fierce pressure from a strong Karen Smyers in 1995, Paula Newby-Fraser stumbled, weaved, and collapsed, postponing an eighth Hawaii Championship until the next year. Tim DeBoom quit 13 miles into the marathon in 2003, kidney stones dooming his shot at a third consecutive crown.

Central to the lore of the Hawaii Ironman is the warning that overconfidence and braggadocio will get you crushed. Veteran triathletes speak candidly about the power and mystique of the Big Island. The place is alive with moist air, thick foliage, gravity-defying geckoes and creepy insects. Only 405,000 years old, Hawaii is both the newest and most isolated place on Earth. It's home to the world's largest volcanic mountain, Mauna Loa, and the world's tallest volcano, Mauna Kea. It has active volcanoes like Kilauea, and lava flows will melt down a neighborhood when given the chance. The most rational triathlete admits a fear of Madame Pele, goddess of the volcanoes, the revered spirit of Hawaiian mythology who has the side-job of bullying triathletes.

According to the story, Pele seduced her sister's husband and her sister "hunted her down like a wild animal," killing her for the betrayal. Pele transmogrified into a goddess, and a rather testy one. It's said she lives in a crater within

Kilauea, where locals and inspired tourists toss her offerings. It's mythology of course, but when the wind is so stiff you're forced to get out of the saddle on a downhill, or you puke for the fourth time, or the chain breaks on a new bike, a skeptic is readily converted.

The Ironman speaks to our desire to be strengthened in a trial by fire. It resists being figured out. After years of sticking in there, Tim DeBoom was rewarded with two World Championships. Allegorically speaking, Madame Pele is curious to see how much DeBoom wants it again. As Don Norcross reported on ironmanlive.com, DeBoom's trial continued well after officials scooped him up and took him to the medical tent. Three weeks after October's race, DeBoom passed more kidney stones. Shortly after that, he broke an elbow in a mountain bike accident. The recovery pain caused DeBoom to grind his teeth at night, and two of his teeth cracked. Root canal surgeries followed.

DeBoom's not the first to suffer the slings and arrows of the Hawaii Ironman obsession, nor will he be the first to fight it off and come back better than ever. There are prices to be paid, and thousands of age group and professional triathletes have gladly paid them. It's what makes the Hawaii Ironman the hardest triathlon in the world, and, oddly enough, the most coveted.

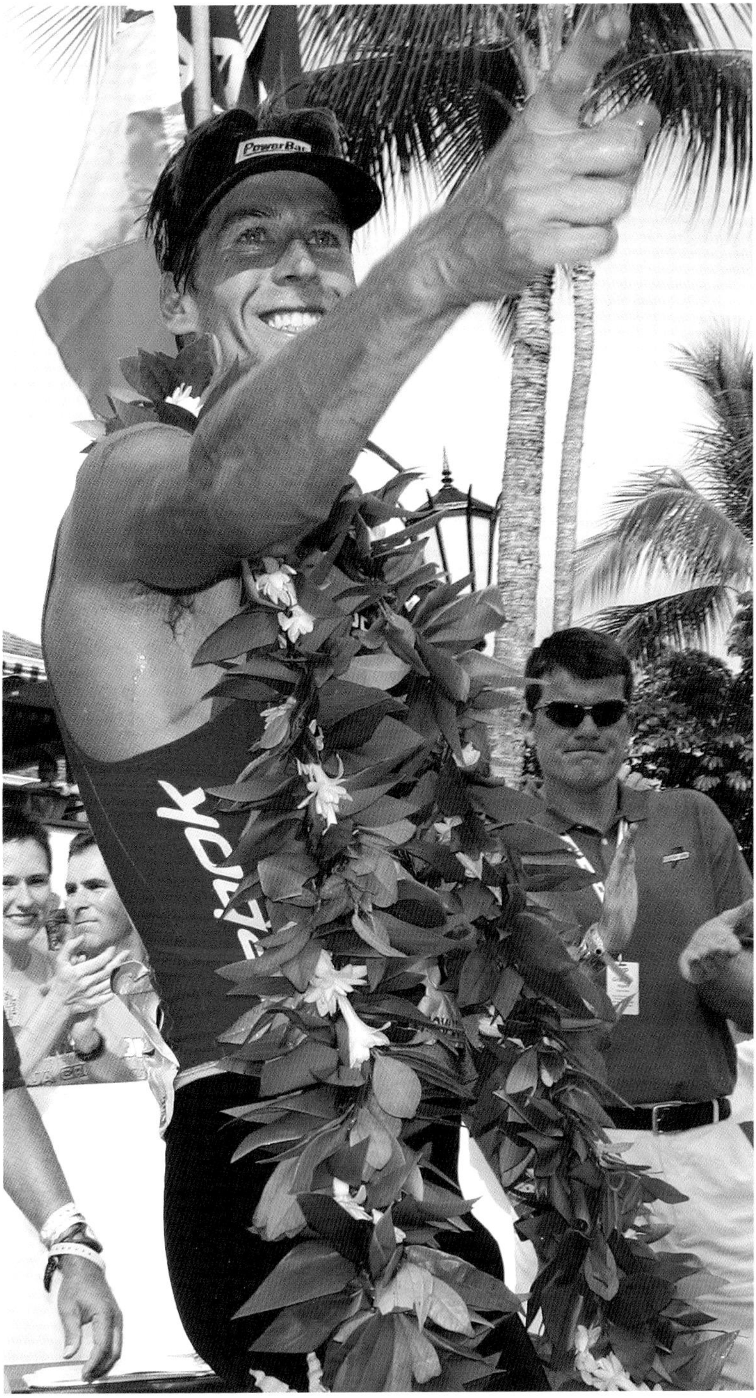
PowerBar

5.2 Making the Time

Look deep into the results from any triathlon, and you see the black and white numbers recorded by the clocks, computers and timing systems. What you don't see are the hundreds and thousands of stories that energize a triathlon with the emotional depth they contain. It's why watching the finish of a long triathlon can mesmerize you for hours. At the 2004 CaliforniaMan Triathlon, more than 300 triathletes took on the adventure of breaking in a new Ironman-length race.

Jerome Beauchamp was 40 years old, a husband and family man with four kids, and, by his own description, getting "chunky" from lack of exercise. "I didn't do anything," he says. "I just worked. All I'd done for 12 years was work." Living in Auburn and working in the real estate business, his last triathlon was a Bud Light Triathlon in 1983.

It was in early summer of 2003 that his return to the sport was prompted, at his 14-year-old daughter's swim practice.

"Steve Casperite was a friend of mine, and he was the seventh grade coach," says Beauchamp. "He talked me into coming to the workout. When I arrived, Steve handed me a swimsuit and implored me to join the workout. I was 187 pounds, 5-foot-11, and I'm looking at this little Speedo — size 32. And so my daughter comes up to me and she's crying, literally crying, begging me not to put on the suit and embarrass her friends. Well, I went ahead and did it. I walk out of the bathroom in the suit, and all the kids stare at me and start cracking up. That's what sent me the message. I knew I had to change my life."

Beauchamp did the workout and later struck up a deal with Casperite to do some real training. It was about then that he heard of the new CaliforniaMan Triathlon in Folsom, an Ironman-length triathlon that was essentially being staged in his backyard.

"That did it," he recalls. "I was thinking about going for Western States, but my knees had been giving me trouble, so CaliforniaMan was perfect."

Casperite, 42, who had completed an Ironman in the early 1980s, became a workout partner and mentor. They established their team, "Middle-Aged Madness," and decided to use the goal of completing CaliforniaMan to raise money for local charities.

"Steve told me that we'd be getting up early, weight training at five and swimming after that. I hadn't gotten up before six in a couple of years. He also said we had to ride all winter," says Beauchamp.

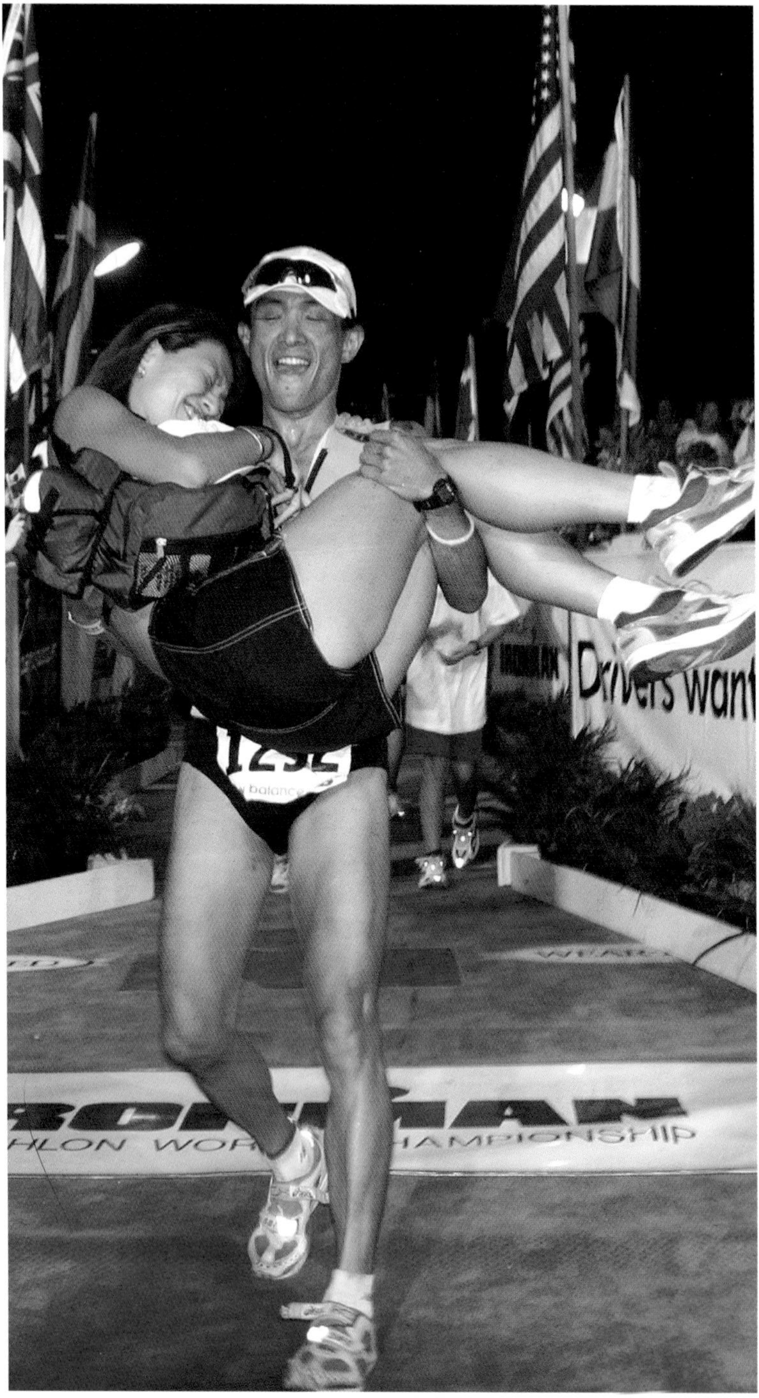
Drivers want

They launched into their bike training with a first ride that seriously tested their resolve. "It was about 29 degrees out, and we didn't have any of the right clothing," Beauchamp says. "On a long downhill, I was just freezing my ass off. My feet were frozen. My hands were frozen. I couldn't even squeeze the brakes. Seriously, I had snot frozen on my face. So, after the ride, we went to Bicycles Plus and bought everything. They showed me these gloves — they looked like ski gloves — and I said, 'Yeah, we need 'em.'"

"And we did it," Beauchamp adds. "We rode all through the winter."

These days, bookstores are filled with fad diets making grand promises of weight loss. But how simple the truth really is: Exercise consistently and you lose unwanted pounds. Beauchamp's year was proof of this: Over the course of his training program, he went from 187 to 164, and in peaking chiseled himself down to 158.

"My fighting weight," he adds.

The morning of the race on May 22, 2004, Beauchamp and Casperite met at 4 am and made their way to the start, along with a thousand others competing in the inaugural CaliforniaMan and the CaliMan Half. The Middle-Aged Madness teammates struck out on the 2.4-mile swim in the spirit of an inter-team competition. Casperite took advantage of his strength in the swim and opened up a six-minute lead, swimming 52:14 to Beauchamp's 58:33.

Casperite continued to expand his lead on the bike.

"I got smoked on the bike," says Beauchamp. "We had a 25 mph wind in our face all day. And Brad Kearns told me to drink a bottle of energy drink, six scoops of it in the bottle, each hour. Man, did I get sick of that stuff. The bike ride was taking me seven hours! When I was getting close to the finish of the bike, I was sick. I was done. I thought no way would I ever be able to do the marathon. No way! The really sick part was that I could time how much Steve was putting on me each loop — three minutes each time."

Casperite was 36 minutes ahead by the end of the bike.

Kearns, a former pro triathlete and Auburn-based coach and race director, talked Beauchamp through the transition. It was a good thing, because no way was he "done". In fact, Beauchamp recalled earlier philosophical advice provided by Kearns through an e-mail.

"He wrote me and said, 'So what if you're scared? No one cares.'"

"I started to eat some food and instantly felt better. I gave Kearns crap about his drink idea and started gorging. I ate M & Ms, cookies and sandwiches."

He also started peeling off sub-nine-minute miles. Even as the race wore down closer to the final miles, he held to his rule of ultra-running: Whatever you do, don't stop. Shuffle if you have to, but don't stop and don't walk.

The loop-style course provided him with a glance of Casperite's position, and he had uncovered the secret value of persistence in an Ironman distance event: No matter how large a lead, they can always come back to you. Casperite's lead had been reduced to five minutes, and the race was on.

"I'm telling you man, it became my life's mission to catch

Steve," says Beauchamp. Then lightning struck in the form of cramps.

"One in my calf and one in my hamstring. I couldn't move my right leg." Beauchamp was forced to stretch for five minutes. "I said 'This cannot be happening!' I had to catch that guy!"

The cramps passed, and soon enough, Casperite was not only within his reach, but standing at an aid station.

"I knew he was hurting. I also knew it was questionable if we were going to be able to break 13 hours."

On the course, Middle-Aged Madness had an emergency meeting and a fire was lit in the spirit of helping each other beat the clock.

"I mean, I'd been training with this guy for months," says Beauchamp. "We'd spent 400 hours together. You really forge a friendship. So it all became about breaking 13 hours together. We had four miles to go, and Steve's knee was killing him."

They broke the remaining distance up, mentally, into one-mile increments and ran and walked with the goal of an 11-minute pace. They gained a minute of cushion by the first of the four miles.

"I got goose bumps," says Beauchamp. "We had just been two couch potatoes who decided to get off our butts, and here we were. And we knew we could do it."

Adrenalin pumping, they clocked an 8:45 mile and clasped hands as they crossed the finish line together,

Casperite in 12:47:26 and Beauchamp in 12:47:27, 77th and 78th in the CaliforniaMan competition.

Having raised $5,000 during a dramatic day that turned out a success, Beauchamp beams when speaking about his story.

"It was all it should have been," he says.

5.3 Finishing Can Be Everything

Careful what you wish for. The cliché was trapped in the revolving door of my mind when a voice, edged with an official sound, snapped up my attention.

"Number 1055. Are you dropping out?"

It was a medical official in khaki shorts and a white polo shirt. I looked up into the glint of sunglasses.

Why would he think I was quitting the race? Just because I was sprawled out on the shoulder of the Queen Ka' ahumanu Highway, on the verge of babbling to myself, socks and cycling shoes looking as if I'd stripped them off my feet and whipped them at a passing helicopter? Because my bike was lying on its side 20 feet away?

How could he ever have come to the conclusion that I was dropping out?

There I was, a participant in the Hawaii Ironman — inarguably the most prestigious event in the sport of triathlon, and an event I'd dreamed about being in for 18 years — lying by the side of the road looking like I was waiting to be rescued by aliens. Most of the Hawaii Ironman's 2.4-miles of ocean swimming, 112-miles of biking, and 26.2-miles of running takes place on this long expanse of lonely road. (Not the ocean swimming, though. That takes place in the ocean.)

The Queen K, as it's commonly referred to, cuts through the lava desert on the northeast side of the Big Island, a black moonscape that slides from Mauna Kea to the Pacific Ocean. This is a post-volcanic world that knows only heat and wind, a landscape without pity — something I felt badly in need of at that moment. My feet were sizzling, my brain scrambled, shoulders sunburned, stomach on strike, and I was not even to the halfway point yet.

My feet were the impetus behind my desire to babble. I felt betrayed. The 2.4-mile swim that I and 1,532 others had started at daybreak from the Kailuha-Kona Bay had been a relatively pleasant experience, except for some chafing and saltwater burn. I changed into cycling clothes, had my body slathered with sun block by four women (one of the highlights of the day), put on a helmet and straddled my 18-speed carbon-fiber road bike.

For 10 miles, the bike ride was charming. A warm sun was out — but not too warm — and the air was still. Great conditions for a long ride. But between mile 9 and 10, the still air was hijacked by 30 mph headwinds, known as the "mumukus," that would be in my face, and everyone else's, for the rest of the northward ride to the small town of Hawi, where we would turn around.

With the prospect of running a marathon in hot and humid conditions, giving everything you've got to putt along at 5 mph on a 112-mile course really sucks. But the topper was that, inexplicably, my feet started burning. They felt like I'd dunked them in a bucket of acid. The harder I pushed on the pedals, the more they burned, and the more the wind blew, the more I needed to press down on the pedals. The finisher's T-shirt felt a decade away.

Now, you expect moments like this when you sign the dotted line and send in the registration fee for an event like this. You might even say that's why you do it in the first place. It's these moments, and the way past competitors have dealt with them, that have given Hawaii its irresistible lure, and it's moments like these that make crossing the finish line — no matter how long it ends up taking — a sweet experience.

I knew all that stuff, and yet the medical official's offer was tempting. If I said yes, he'd help me to my feet and walk me to the white van that sat idling 10 yards away from me. I'd crawl in the back and nab a root beer from a Styrofoam cooler, and guzzle it down in an air-conditioned environment. He'd drive me into downtown Kona, where I could shower, put on coral blue beach shorts and massage sandals and spend the rest of the day drinking mai-tais from an open-air bar and watching hundreds of triathletes from around the world exult as they crossed the finish line. Exulting because they hadn't given in to the temptation I had fallen victim to.

Later on, I would realize that it was a rookie mistake I'd made the day before that put me in this predicament: After a quick dip in the ocean, I climbed the stairs from the beach to the parking lot and stopped to talk to a couple of friends. I didn't take the time to put on shoes, nor had I taken the time to notice that I was standing on hot pavement.

It only took five minutes to burn off enough skin to plant a land mine for the next day's race. Four months of training versus five minutes of blithe stupidity. The result was a signature Hawaii Ironman problem, as I was left without the slightest foothold on which to anchor an excuse to quit. The burning sensation was irritating, but it posed no threat of permanent damage. It was simply going to make the rest of the race even more uncomfortable than it was already going to be.

The really annoying thing was that "overcoming the pain" and finishing with feet burned from standing in a parking lot doesn't make for good bragging material. How pathetic would it sound to say, "Hey guys, I finished the Hawaii Ironman, despite my burning feet!"

But in my own private universe, this was my albatross, the single prize being the knowledge that I didn't give up. I was also aware that each and every one of my fellow competitors were having their own troubles. We were all screwed. Pushed at some point in the day to our own internal brinks, each one of us would face the question, "Why am I doing this to myself?"

An outstanding question. If you're reading this book, I'll wager that you already know that if you don't run into this question on occasion, you might not be working hard enough. You answer the question by recalling the weeks, months and years of preparation, the series of goals that you've accomplished, each one taking you to the next level of physical and mental development, each one requiring significant amounts of sacrifice and discomfort.

This was exactly why I was in the 2000 Hawaii Ironman, and why, over the course of the past 12 years of my life, I have felt the need to subject myself to periodic litmus tests. There truly is no finish line.

It was June of that year when I realized I needed another wake-up call. I was sitting on the edge of a mattress in the room I'd rented in Brooklyn — having relocated to New York from California — late on a Saturday morning. In the preceding weeks, I'd fallen victim to vulturous thoughts hatched from the confusion surrounding a fractured relationship, and there I was, dazed and stuck in the past.

I was hungry and had nothing to eat, so I dug up two dollars and walked to a corner gas station. I bought a container of yogurt with strawberries at the bottom. I walked back to my room and set down the yogurt. I peeled off the lid and stared at it, remembering then that I didn't have a spoon.

I froze. I felt no impulse to move. I wondered if I would ever move again. It seemed very possible that I might spend the rest of the day staring at a cup of Dannon yogurt,

perfectly inert. Up until that point, I wasn't sure I was going to accept a lottery slot to race in the Hawaii Ironman that I'd drawn a few months before, but after staring at the yogurt for an hour, I realized I needed to challenge myself again and wake myself out of my depressed stupor.

Training for and racing the Hawaii Ironman was the right type of impetus to get me back into motion, and it was something I'd wanted to do for 18 years.

The Hawaii Ironman was in its fourth year of existence when the dramatic finish of Julie Moss, a lifeguard from San Diego, California, was broadcast on ABC's *Wide World of Sports*. Moss was leading the women at the end of the February 1982 event. Then, in the final stages of the marathon run, well after sunset, her body fell apart.

Her leg muscles gave out, as did her control of body functions, but she continued to move toward the finish, at first wobbling from side to side across the road, then collapsing into a crawl on her hands and knees.

All the while, she persistently refused offers of help from spectators and race officials. Even though Kathleen McCartney passed her for the win, it was the heroic image of Moss' will to finish that electrified the television audience.

Ironically, despite the disturbing amount of duress Moss was filmed enduring, interest in doing the race exploded. Except for the small reserve of lottery slots that are given out each year, the only way to get to the starting line of the Hawaii Ironman today is to win a slot at one of the qualifying triathlons that are held across the United States and throughout the world, including locations in South Africa, Brazil, Malaysia, and Europe.

My fascination with the sport was originally ignited by the courage displayed by Moss, but as the years went by, many more stories of heroism sprang from the event, and I never missed out on watching the race.

On the elite level, Mark Allen's journey was a seven-year testament to the value of perseverance. Having been inspired by Moss' finish as well, Allen — also from San Diego — raced for the win in six Hawaii Ironmans leading up to 1989, often in contention through the bike and into the run. It was in the run that he routinely crumbled, usually losing to Dave Scott of Davis, California, who ended up winning the race a masterful six times.

Allen, on the other hand, suffered physical breakdown after physical breakdown, once even being carted off with internal bleeding. It was in 1989 that Allen finally put all the pieces together and, in one of the most dramatic endurance competitions ever recorded, ran stride for stride with Scott through the marathon.

Pushing each other into otherworldly levels of pain that were clearly registered in the anguish on their faces, the two ran at nearly a six-minute-mile pace through vicious heat and humidity. With only two miles to go, Allen made a surge that Scott could not respond to, and broke away for a slender win in a record time, finishing the marathon leg in a jaw-dropping 2:40:04.

As dramatic as the Allen-Scott duel was, there have always been equally, if not more, sensational stories well behind the first place finishers.

A father, Dick Hoyt, who powered both himself and his paraplegic son, Richard, through the entire race; John Maclean of Australia, who became the first physically challenged athlete to finish the event by powering a hand-crank bike and wheelchair in an official finish; former NFL lineman Darryl Haley — all 6'5", 300-pounds of him — who finished the race in 1995; and athletes like the late Jim Ward, who became the first 80-year-old to take on the Hawaii Ironman in 1997, and Sister Madonna Buder, a nun who toed the line in the year 2000 at the age of 70.

No excuses. By comparison, my hot feet seemed pretty silly, and I had to laugh at myself after the official asked me if I was going to drop out. It was good to laugh, even though I knew that the next seven hours of my life would be uncomfortable ones. In fact, they would be even more uncomfortable than I anticipated.

At the bike turnaround I, and those around me, would find that the winds turned at the same time, crushing our hopes to soar back to town on a tailwind. The last four hours were spent dealing with cramping muscles and a testy stomach aggravated by 26 miles of pounding the pavement.

While running on the Queen K Highway, I would have an open view of a spectacular sunset, and from there on out, certain that I was going to finish, I would work to memorize every sight, sound and chill. I would run down Ali'i Drive through a cheering and dancing crowd and cross the finish line, where friends would be waiting to take me out for hamburgers that I would barely be able to eat.

I knew that something like that was waiting for me should I decide to get off my butt and begin paying the price. To be honest, the decision to endure everything that I would have to endure had already been made. It's just that I'd needed a moment to dust off the reasons behind my being there, knowing, deep down, how much the reward for finishing meant.

Perspective

THE JOURNEY OF JIM MACLAREN

When able-bodied triathletes and triathlon fans see a wheelchair triathlete round the last corner, finish-line applause lifts to an emotional pitch. We want them to know how much we respect what they've overcome and what they're doing.

But this is where we usually draw the line in thinking about it. We may know firsthand about the rigors of being an Ironman, but it's impossible to meaningfully imagine life, training and racing in the physically challenged division. Maybe we don't think deeper on it because we know it would be ridiculously presumptuous; maybe we don't think about it because every time we're out on a long bike ride, there's a close call with a pickup truck and we can't deny the fact that over the edge of the definition of close call is a world where being paraplegic is lucky. Maybe we just don't know what to say.

The uneasiness triathletes feel was illustrated when Jim MacLaren gave a speech at the Hawaii Ironman after a second life-changing accident. In the first, he'd lost a leg after he was hit by a bus when he was on his motorcycle in New York. Then when he was 30, during the bike leg of a San Diego triathlon, he was struck by a van when crossing an intersection. He broke his neck and was left quadriplegic.

Elizabeth Gilbert, in a compelling article on MacLaren published in *GQ*, chronicled the moment:

About a year after his accident, he made a difficult voyage to Hawaii to speak before a convention of Ironman athletes. He was wheeled out onstage to a standing ovation. When the applause finally died down, Jim began with, of all things, a dark joke: 'For years I sat out there in that audience and listened to the best Ironman champions in the world speak from this very podium. I always wondered what it would take for a guy like me to be invited up here. I never realized it would be so simple — all I had to do was break my neck.'

There was a bone-chilling silence.

Jim thought, 'Whoops...'

Within the article, Gilbert detailed the agonies, both physical and mental, that MacLaren had suffered through. How it was far from over, and how it's never over. You only begin to see the strength and endurance of Jim MacLaren in how he painstakingly works it out in his head on a daily basis. Seeing so deeply into his situation he *knows* what happened to him was an extreme case of a blessing in disguise.

Two-time PC division champ Carlos Moleda talked about the same struggle. "I have mornings where I wake up and it's like, '*Damn*, I want to go for a run.'"

It's fair to say, albeit from a distance, that physically disabled athletes are on the most intimate terms with the ultimate personal goal of the Ironman: self-knowledge. It's fun to hear the cheers and to blow a few minds in the workplace when you tell them about what you were up to last weekend in Lake Placid.

But we know the real value, the real stuff, lies in driving ourselves through the low moments of an Ironman, past the inner voice egging us on to quit. It's in these times we get a glimpse of our own weaknesses and strengths, and maybe a bit of real understanding about fighting the great daily fight in the physically challenged division.

The day I first witnessed the athletic drama that unfolds in the PC division was in Lubbock, Texas, during a June heat wave in the late 1990s. I'd interviewed the winners of the Buffalo Springs Lake Half-Ironman and was finishing up my day's work by taking some photos out on the course.

It was a 110-degree day. At least. It was the kind of heat that melts the life out of you the moment you walk out of the air-conditioning. Triathletes were making it to the finish line thanks to race directors Mike and Marti Greer's wizardry in making ice stay ice under the fire of fierce temperatures. Still, watching the athletes survive the day was one of the more awesome displays I had witnessed as a triathlon journalist.

But the most awesome was yet to come. With a sun burning as if it was 100 feet above, I was standing near the top of a steep climb on the run course. The Greers take delight in surprising out-of-towners with the truth about West Texas: it's flat, but not *all* flat. This particular climb was wicked steep, and the blacktop, the black cooked out of it, burned to stand on right through your shoes. But with my attention caught by the strain of two athletes, both climbing up the hill in wheelchairs, I didn't feel a thing.

The angle of the incline made it so the panting athletes lost sizeable chunks of ground after each push, in the brief instant they were forced to release their grip on the hand rims. The stillness of the day made it like breathing inside a hot-air balloon, and they rasped for oxygen. Yet, they weren't just lasting out the hill, they were racing each other for a slot to the Hawaii Ironman.

Until that moment, I really hadn't paid much attention to the division. If you're watching an Ironman, usually your attention is focused on the drama at the front of the race, and within that, you have a good idea about what the rest of the pack is going through. It's easy to give only a glancing thought to the journey wheelchair athletes have made just to get to the starting line. In interviews with competitors like Willie Stewart, an above-the-elbow amputee, who lost most of his arm in a construction accident, becoming a PC triathlete isn't something they jump into after leaving the hospital.

"The two years after the accident, I didn't do a thing," Stewart said. "I had to face my own preconceptions of what it meant to be disabled. I figured since I'd lost my arm that I was destined to just be an office boy somewhere. But things changed when I found the confidence I needed to be seen in public."

David Bailey, a world-class motorcycle racer before he was paralyzed in a bike accident, said he too went through the same sort of psychological ordeal.

The man who would become Bailey's chief rival, Moleda, a Navy SEAL, paralyzed after he was shot in combat, first had to get through nine months of intense rehabilitation before he could even start thinking about any type of comeback in a wheelchair.

After coming to grips with things and deciding to revive the athlete within, things only get tougher. Stewart, for example, decided he wanted to do a Half-Ironman, and had to figure out how to swim.

"The first time I got in the pool, it was ridiculous. I barely made it to the other end. When I got there I said, "How in the hell am I going to swim 1.2 miles?" And using a handcycle and wheelchair in the heat of competition — heat both literal and figurative — becomes an especially daunting task when the road curls upward. In 1994, Australia's John McLean, the first physically challenged athlete to beat the strict bike cut-off time at the Hawaii Ironman, did so after Palani Hill caused him to throw up three times.

When Moleda — who would win two division championships in Hawaii — first started training for the Ironman, he was dumbstruck. After finishing 100-mile training rides, he'd sit, stunned, pouring water over his head and feeling "half-dead."

Bailey tells a story about finishing one of his more demanding brick workouts in San Diego, in preparation for his 3rd clash with Moleda. He was so worked that when drivers honked their horns at him in encouragement, he thought "Shut up. Just leave me alone."

It's easy to rubber stamp the stories that come out of the physically challenged division as "inspirational" and leave it at that. But there's a great deal we can learn from our fellow athletes who've had to improvise an altered version of triathlon. For one thing, if mental strength is the foundation for success in the Ironman, these are the masters.

David Bailey's and Carlos Moleda's three-year battle in Hawaii was proof of this. For another thing — and perhaps most importantly — to squeeze meaning out of triathlon and to keep our egos and perspectives in check, we can learn a lot from the words of MacLaren and the others. Like in MacLaren's explanation to *GQ* of how he came to terms with his disability:

"I have honestly come to believe that I needed these accidents in my life. I completely believe that. Not in terms of paying dues or getting punished by God, but in terms of getting my attention and bringing me deeper inside myself to a place where I could find honesty and peace. Was it destined? Did I literally choose to have these awful things happen to me? No, not in so many words, I don't believe so. But I do believe this — I believe I was born begging for experiences that would show me who I really am. And that's what I've been given."

The Author

T. J. Murphy is the editor of *Triathlete Magazine* and a longtime correspondent for Ironmanlive.com. A four-time Ironman finisher, he's also the co-author of the book *Start to Finish: Ironman Training, 24 Weeks to an Endurance Triathlon*.

Photo Credits

Photos: Robert Murphy
                                   Bakke-Svensson/WTC
                                   Chapter 3.5: Jay Prasuhn
Coverphoto: Bakke-Svensson/WTC
Coverdesign: Jens Vogelsang

Ironman Edition

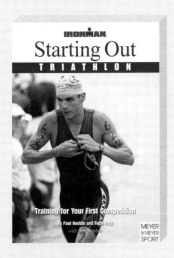

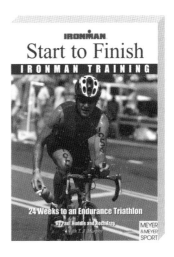

Ironman Edition
Huddle/Frey with Babbitt

Triathlon
– Starting out
Training for Your First Competition

Here's the best book on the market to get you to the starting line. Roch Frey and Paul Huddle are the two most respected names in multi-sport coaching. They cover all the bases in the first book of the Ironman Training Series. Besides running, cycling and swimming, you'll find information on everything from weight training to flexibility to nutrition. Don't sit on the sidelines any longer. With Roch and Paul at your side, anyone and everyone can do a triathlon.

160 pages, full-color print
81 photos, 16 tables
Paperback, 5³/4″ x 8¹/4″
ISBN: 1-84126-101-7
£ 12.95 UK / $ 17.95 US
$ 25.95 CDN / € 16.90

Ironman Edition
Huddle/Frey with Murphy

Start to Finish
Ironman Training:
24 Weeks to an Endurance Triathlon

Okay, you've finished your first short-distance triathlon. Now it's time to up the ante and go further and faster. Paul and Roch are up to the challenge. Longer workouts, balancing work, family and training, adding speed work, recovery and the mental game are all essential when you decide to move up to the Ironman distance. No one has more training or racing experience than Roch and Paul. They will get you to your target race healthy, happy and ready for more. Guaranteed.

178 pages, full-color print
52 photos, 5 tables
Paperback, 5³/4″ x 8¹/4″
ISBN: 1-84126-102-5
£ 12.95 UK / $ 17.95 US
$ 25.95 CDN / € 16.90

MEYER & MEYER Sport | sales@m-m-sports.com | www.m-m-sports.com

MEYER
& MEYER
SPORT

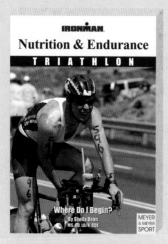

Sheila Dean

Nutrition & Endurance
Where Do I Begin?

With the busy pace of our modern lifestyle, athletes, whether amateurs or professionals, want the latest information on sports nutrition and they want it NOW! Clearly, what is needed are qualified health professionals who can disseminate scientifically substantiated information on sports nutrition.

This book is a guide to healthy eating for anyone who wants to lead a healthier life. Part one is an introduction to basic nutrition and shows you how to go from a poor diet to a healthy diet, while part two transitions the reader into what needs to be done to actually eat for training and competition.

144 pages, full-color print
36 photos, paperback, 5$^{3}/_{4}$" x 8$^{1}/_{4}$"
ISBN 1-84126-105-X
£ 12.95 UK / $ 17.95 US
$ 25.95 CDN / e 16.90

About the edition

The name "Ironman" guarantees expertise in the field of triathlon and endurance sport. The year 2003 marked the 25th anniversary of this magical event that started with a couple of participants and has now grown to be one of the most popular events and also brand names in sports. Starting from this anniversary year, Meyer & Meyer Sport is the exclusive publisher for the World Triathlon Corporation with a whole book series, ranging from the best triathlon training to general health and fitness themes.

Renowned authors, Ironman athletes and legends guarantee that the spirit of Ironman will come to you in the form of a collection of fascinating books.

MEYER
& MEYER
SPORT

MEYER & MEYER Sport | sales@m-m-sports.com | www.m-m-sports.com

25 Legendary Years

Bob Babbitt

25 YEARS OF THE IRONMAN TRIATHLON WORLD CHAMPIONSHIP

Ironman Hall of Fame Inductee Bob Babbitt and some of the world's best photographers lovingly share images and stories from what many consider to be the Toughest Day in Sport, the Ironman.

With a foreword from legendary sportscaster Jim Lampley and an introduction from Ironman creator Commander John Collins, this beautiful book chronicles an event that started out with 15 crazy entrants in 1978 and now, 25 years later, is considered the ultimate goal for athletes worldwide and the ultimate showcase for endurance sports.

2nd, updated edition
Color-photo illustration throughout
200 pages, Hardcover, 10" x 10"
ISBN 1-84126-100-9
£ 19.95 UK / $ 29.95 US
$ 47.95 CDN / € 29.90

MEYER & MEYER Sport | sales@m-m-sports.com | www.m-m-sports.com

Anz Itornkids 06/03

MEYER
& MEYER
SPORT